What did you a Granny?

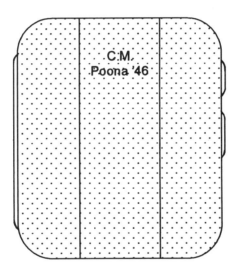

C.M.
Poona '46

Constance Bradford

The illustration is of the inscribed cigarette case given to the author by patients in the hospital in Poona

ISBN 0 952193973

Published by Hunnyhill Publications
Corner Cottage Hunnyhill Brighstone Isle of Wight PO30 4DU
Tel. 01983 740363 email elizabethh@bigwig.net www.bigwig.net/books

Printed by Biltmore Printers Cross Street Newport Isle of Wight

CONTENTS

Introduction

I was born Constance Mary Morgan, in a small mining village in Glamorgan, South Wales in 1918, the last of a family of three girls and three boys. I arrived after a gap of nine years. This made me a lonely child as my eldest sister was already seventeen at my birth. The poverty was acute at the end of the First World War particularly in the industrial areas. All the people were coping with a frugal existence. Fortunately my father kept us well stocked with game, fish was plentiful and our two large vegetable gardens were very productive.

My motive for writing this epistle is purely to help the younger members of our society today to understand the discipline of service as we knew it This is written entirely from memory as we were forbidden to keep diaries or have cameras.

The united spirit of Britain in defence of our country was total and so it could be today if it was left to the British people. But truth is undermined by politics, money and so-called sexual freedom. Without discipline nothing is of any worth.

I want my family to know what Granny did in the war.

Isle of Wight 2001

Acknowledgements

Firstly my husband, Donald who enjoyed some of the rough script before his illness.

To my daughter, Susan for recovering 'India' when it disappeared from my computer and my daughter, Joanna for her patience in straightening out my early computer struggles.

To my *many* friends who have encouraged and supported me in my small effort and to Elizabeth Hutchings for rescuing me and getting the ball rolling and publishing the result of my labours.

Autumn 1938

There was the terrible threat from Germany with the news of their immense armies. Thankfully we were in complete ignorance of their intense brutality, nevertheless the hate for bullies made us prepared to face up to our enemies.

Not wishing to wait for a call up I decided to take nursing training, which was very demanding and of the 'old school.' Everyone lived in a 'Nurses Home.' Sisters and the matrons had their own quarters. If a nurse married she left the service. The sister in charge of a ward had her desk at the entrance of the ward where she could see all the activities while charting the patients' case notes and being available to the staff and checking on the patients' treatments. The training was hard but learning the ability to care for sick people was the prime factor.

It was a happy time in spite of our hard work. We had a profession to be proud of and were taught well. None of the familiarities of today were necessary and are not an advantage in any case.

We worked for a pittance compared with today's rates, that not being the object of the exercise. For the first six months of the war we had no bombing, but following the London pattern we in Manchester started experiencing vicious bombing. With German efficiency the moment the six o'clock news was switched on the sirens would start their howling. Again at precisely six am they would depart. After all the tension the patients would be urgently needing bed pans and a hectic demand ensued.

The only defences against the bombers overhead were mobile naval guns that ran up and down on the main road on one length of the hospital. Unfortunately they were useless potting any aeroplanes but the noise they made would frighten an enemy. The Messerschmitts and Heinkels were safe from them.

All the time I was there none of us ever entered an air raid shelter, but we did fire watching on the roof on the fifth floor for firebombs. This was even more terrifying.

This was a very large hospital, strategically placed as behind us was an important railway, alongside that was a very important engineering works, Vickers Armstrong, which ran for a quarter of a mile. To cap it all the Manchester Ship Canal on moonlit nights made a perfect pathway for the bombers. We could not have been in a more conspicuous place.

I found the north country accent another nightmare as I had to take all telephone messages which completely floored me at times and I found it exceptionally difficult. As only a three-month junior I was sent to work in the operating theatre, where my principal job was to count the swabs which came in rapid succession from over the shoulders of the surgeon and in all directions. Dressed in theatre gown, mask etc. searching over the floor for these blood-soaked swabs, with a piece of chalk in my hand to write down the numbers on the board with him calling out, 'How many is that now?' through his mask and a muffled broad Scottish accent I found this also a positive nightmare. It could have made a very funny film.

The theatre sister was a very kind Irish lady who explained to the 'great man' that this was my first morning in theatre. His remark was that I should have fainted by now as most new people did. I could have replied that I had been too busy looking for his swabs! I said my prayers diligently that night in the hope that the swabs were correct.

The air raids continuing we, the whole theatre staff, doctors, sisters, staff nurses and juniors slept on the floor of the theatre entrance without mattresses, in trousers and jerseys and only our cloaks to cover us. We could not take the risk of going to our rooms with the possibility of our return being blocked by the debris of a hit.

By this time we were used to sleeping anywhere and working sixteen hours a day with lectures in our off duty time where I inevitably fell asleep, awaking suddenly to find my pen had found its way across the page. Coming to final exams I set my alarm on for 4am and by putting my window up I studied or two hours, the cold air keeping me awake.

My sister, Elizabeth and her little family lived opposite the hospital and I hated them living alone, her husband, a doctor being in the North African campaign, for the air raids were intense. They had steel girders installed in the cellar, with sleeping bunks. I did go over to sleep there as often as I dared, which was not allowed, but with the constant confusion the gate porters were kind and understanding.

On December 23 1940 I happened to be with the family when there was a gigantic bomb which made the steel supports move. It was nearing 6am and the end of the raid and I went over the road to report on duty only to find the hospital had taken a direct hit from a land mine. The high tower with the administration was destroyed with our wonderful Doctor Giles, our chief, and matron and several more devoted people killed. All other parts of this huge building were badly affected. Windows in bathrooms went at the same time and nurses in the corridors were blown by blast.

That night two thousand people were made homeless. The roads were filled with people distressed, pushing handcarts with the remains of their belongings. The theatre was filled with people in severe shock, big strong policemen weeping uncontrollably, so little one could do, how could they be consoled?

That winter everywhere was so cold. The miracle was we had hot water so we had speedy baths in windowless bathrooms. Our food was meagre to say the least and we were hungry. The great day came when we had an egg, the first in six months. The senior staff, I know fared better.

My friends and I were coming up to our final exams, always an anxious time for everyone. I was given much encouragement by our Sister Tutor and found the papers touched on subjects I knew. The examiner for the practical was the famous Evelyn Pearce from whose textbooks we had studied. She was so very nice.

In spite of all the bombing harassment we got to the theatre to see some of the finest shows by Ivor Novello and Noel Coward, first nights before they went on to London; Sunday afternoon concerts by the Halle Orchestra under Sir John Barbarolli; first rate films, some five hours long such as 'Gone with the Wind' when all patrons were asked

3

to come to the stalls when the bombing became a little more dangerous. It was so wonderful to have quality entertainment at such a time.

With my finals successfully completed I decided to follow my sister and her family. Her eight-year-old daughter had contracted the early signs of tuberculosis and was in a special hospital for three months' treatment to be followed by moving to the coast of North Wales for the remainder of the war. I then worked in a hospital in Abergelie in order to be near her.

I did my work to the best of my ability in this hospital and for the first time began to realise that the animosity of the north Welsh against the south was very bitter indeed. I found them so mean and narrow-minded and untouched by the war. We had to walk five miles from the train to the hospital and cars would pass but never once in the eighteen months was I offered a lift. This was most unusual in those days as everyone helped each other. All over the country there was this wonderful camaraderie in a united nation.

My sister and family became more settled and that was when I decided to apply for the services.

Queen Alexandra's Nursing Service

Having applied to this service and being accepted as a wartime Sister, or Reserve, known then as the Ladies of the Army Nursing Service, and soon changed, unknown to us. I was given the rank of Lieutenant. It is now the Queen Alexandra's 1`Royal Army Nursing Corps.

At my first posting I was sent to Hatfield House, Hertfordshire, that magnificent historic and romantic place, bursting at that time with spring and all the lovely flowers and the grandeur of the Elizabethan building. It took little imagination to see the young Elizabeth walking with her ladies, or playing games with much laughter and gaiety under the great and magnificent oaks. The grounds were extensive with unkempt lawns now in wartime conditions. Nevertheless it was a great privilege to be here. How old were the oaks I wondered as I sat under the one that Elizabeth was supposed to have when given the news of her accession? Her imprisonment was in the earlier and smaller building, with a thatch roof.

The huge house had been given to the Army for a military hospital for wartime. This is where I met up with forty-five nursing sisters, mostly in their twenties, who had come from all over Britain. Speaking for myself coming to the country after the intense bombing of the cities was an immense relief.

All information was withheld and secret. We attended the patients, discussed wild rumours and were introduced to Army drill, which came to us as a great shock as we were quite unprepared for it. This was a new idea the Army had thought up, deciding to convert us into soldiers; what a mistake that was. It must have been a heartbreaking sight to a military observer, to say nothing of the Sergeant Major, who with tongue in cheek tried to teach us to march and salute, which none of us had ever done before. It was chaotic.

Working in these lovely surroundings with rooms so spacious, with the walls of wood panelling, no high dusting was permitted. Battle honour flags, just out of reach and coated with black dust nevertheless hung over the beds. But for the protective covers they would have disintegrated at a touch! So much for asepsis

I very much enjoyed visiting the roof with its fascinating period chimneys, which I called terracotta barley sticks, twisted and not all the same style, very tall with beautiful Tudor designs, grouped together in different areas over this great roof. There was a low doorway at the base of one edifice where a figure in Elizabethan court dress had been seen standing motionless by some of the staff but sadly I never had the privilege.

While on night duty I used to watch the bombers fly overhead leaving after sunset for Germany, my prayers went with them. This sight and roar overhead brought one back to the present day with a jolt. The reality was even more forceful at dawn, a faint rumble was heard in the distance and with sinking heart I inevitably went again to see the return of the bombers only to witness the vacant spaces in the formations, heartbreaking.

Returning from shopping in the town one day, complete with parcels, I was very smartly saluted by two other ranks. This came as a surprise and in my return I made a poor attempt very nearly dropping my parcels which of course must have caused the chaps some amusement. I realised the necessity to learn my drill and also realised that carrying of parcels was frowned upon.

We continued to enjoy our lovely surroundings for a whole six weeks when, without warning we were assembled to meet the Matron, Miss Ivers and Under Matron, Miss Richardson with whom we were to remain as a unit. At the same time we were issued with tropical kit with a warning of absolute secrecy. We were not permitted to write to friends or relations at all as this would endanger ourselves but also thousands of others. This was observed very seriously. We weren't told anything more but we all respected the silence and the need for it.

From that moment on all 'passes' for the town were suspended and Miss Ivers called us together informing us to complete our packing and collect a small packet of food and drink as we should be leaving in an hour.

At dusk we assembled in the hospital square and climbed into enclosed trucks, bidding a silent farewell to this historic place and grateful to have had the privilege and liberty of getting to know it.

Of course we were full of anticipation, looking forward to whatever new experience was in store. All we guessed was that we were out for the night at least.

All was pitch dark in the town and country in those days when one could really appreciate the night sky, seeing many more stars than nowadays with their formations so clear. Our lorries were slowing down. Jumping down from the trucks we found ourselves in the goods yard of a railway station. We made a 'follow my leader' onto the platform in silence. With darkness all around, the train awaiting us also silent and dark, no other people, no name of the station and no chatter, just the crunch of our feet.

At this particular time, if ever a stranger were to ask local people the name of a station it always raised suspicion. Several reports were given to the police by local people when strangers were noticed. We seemed to be the only passengers for some time, making wild guesses about our destination and some quiet fun. A rattle of heavy chains with some jolting made us realise more trains were being hitched onto ours, while shuffling feet were heard with sounds of equipment carried by troops trying to get into carriages.

Trains and shining railway lines were easily spotted from the air on moonlit nights. Then there was always a glow from the firebox from the two engines creating the steam that the fireman in the driver's cabin was responsible for. They were dedicated men who lived for their engines, arriving and leaving on the dot of the minute, with great pride, alas not so the trains of today.

Hearing more shunting plus hitching on of more carriages it dawned on us we were growing into some huge troop train. Travelling through the night making several stops, we were obviously picking up more troops on the way until even the corridors were full. The train was still in darkness and as quiet as was possible, the only light was the reflection into the night sky where the fires of the two engines pulling and pushing this immense load. This was some train.

As dawn came we saw hills and mountains with wonderful country but there was nothing to indicate where we were. Eventually the sea came into view, which was no surprise, having packed tropical kit. The platform was almost along the dockside, a mass of shipping all around, but one much larger vessel than the others was awaiting us, the New Zealand cruiser the Rangitata.

Being privileged to be first on board gave us a chance to view the land from the top deck of this great ship. Some of my colleagues were Scots but failed to recognise their own country but having been to Dunoon the previous year I was able to name it at once.

We spent the whole day watching the activities on the dock, with the many hundreds of service personnel, Army, Navy and Air Force, including Canadians, New Zealand Air Force, Australian Air Force, Turkish Officers, who were neutral in the war at that time. Two ballet companies concluded the list as far as we knew.

The Senior Staff, as was expected had the first class cabins on the top deck. We, although there were three-tiered bunks wherever possible, were above the waterline and boasted a porthole.

We assembled at various times for instructions from either of the Matrons, but were not required to work. We were all under thirty and from training schools all over Britain. One or two were very newly trained though others had done four or five, some even six years training.

Over the horizon we heard, on the grapevine, the convoy was assembled. Some smaller naval vessels such as corvettes were near round about us and we were quite excited with so much going on. These waters had been especially bad for shipping, many ships having been lost in the North Atlantic to German subs.

On waking in the morning we were conscious of the throb of our engines. Getting dressed we eagerly made our way to the nearest deck to view the activities of the Naval escort. It was an incredible sight of huge battleships, cruisers and vessels we were ignorant of. More of the convoy we were told was over the horizon.

Daily life on board was very entertaining, chatting with groups of people, all having their own ideas as to where this convoy was taking us. The sea was calm and this was a very crowded ship. There were an enormous number of troops in their three-tiered hammocks and sometimes four-layers we were told. Below the waterline must have been air-conditioned. This was also occupied by the male dancers of the Ballet Company.

Having had our daily meeting with Matron we were given some limited information that amounted to, 'We were progressing well bearing south towards the West African coast.'

As evening approached on the first day, I remember it so well, people fell silent on deck and slowly as everyone realised the danger of our situation the silence of the engine seemed to saturate the whole ship. Soon we were quite alone in this vast ocean seeing the magnificent escort disappearing over the horizon. We were told to check life belts and keep them with us and to gather essential items for panic bags to be assembled and in case of attack to attach them to our belts should we have to jump. All these instructions were given at the first boat drill that afternoon. We wore trousers and lay on our bunks. Our panic bags consisted of water, chocolate and head cover.

At around midnight, we heard, with much gratitude, the slow thud of our engines. In half a day we rejoined the convoy with thankful hearts hoping never to repeat that little excitement.

Something happens to human behaviour on board ship and is notoriously unaccountable, as anyone with this experience will confirm. Already gossip was in vogue. We enjoyed the Ballet Company on deck taking their exercises that took place throughout the day, having to share the large deck with so many people.

Some amusing gossip came from below deck of the troops who were so unused to men who took dancing of this kind so seriously. Their wearing hairnets to go to bed plus the affectionate terms with which they greeted each other. This must have been sweet really but a rare

9

experience for the average 'Tommy' to take on board in those days.

Still in trouble the engines stopped twice more. Again we chased after the convoy. When we were much further on with our journey we were informed that the whole contingent had zigzagged across the Atlantic more than once, almost to America, dodging the German subs.

By this time we were approaching tropical waters but had been told very little more about our journey. Heading for Freetown we were told we would remain offshore for two days but no shore visit of course. By now we had been at sea about two weeks.

Sometimes the sea became very rough and there was much more space in the dining mess. Not being one to be seasick I rather enjoyed going up on deck. Feeling the wind tearing at my greatcoat and turning my back to it I would be pushed so hard and forced to run to the rise and fall of the vessel.

I especially remember when 'crossing the line' the seas were so rough and it was so cold that not only did I wear my winter suit but also my greatcoat. No ceremony on that occasion for the crossing!

Later the climate changed, everyone's particular unit ordered tropical kit the 'Order of the Day.' We looked smart in ours which was white drill with red flashes of rank. The men too in shorts and long socks and open-necked shirts revealing rather white knees, arms and necks.

There was notorious gossip buzzing around the decks as can be imagined amongst so many thousands of young people. Eventually it spread to the whole convoy. We got to hear of a daily newsletter that was eagerly read and made available to the entire Navy from battleships down to the corvettes. No doubt spiced imaginations had free range too. The inquisitive Corvettes spent much time sailing around our great ship and we enjoyed their obvious interest but soon realised this was where they picked up their gossip to print.

There were also several cargo ships of importance in this huge convoy, but staffed by regular Merchant Navy crews who lacked the spice of such a varied selection of human beings. There was an energetic group who organised certain forms of entertainment to which we were designated. One of which I would gladly have avoided, Housey-housey, which has become immensely popular nowadays as Bingo. There were impromptu talks, the usual card games with people making up Bridge fours, but definitely no gambling. There was also daily boat drill at our regular stations with strict inspections improving our speed and efficiency and taken very seriously.

Occasionally there were unfortunate disagreements between the different nationalities. Heated arguments were usually scotched but one of these, which I happened to witness, became quite serious. It could have become an international embarrassment and had to be managed by the Captain. The incident happened as I was coming out of the bar behind a few Australian officers who suddenly stopped to look down on some Turkish officers who were going down a companionway and the Australians, with a derogatory word spat on them.

It happened to be a sensitive time in the war as Mr Churchill was trying to encourage Turkey, which was neutral to support the British. This created a problem, as the unacceptable words accompanied with the spitting were understood fully by the high-ranking Turkish officers.

The Captain and his high-ranking officers negotiated this successfully in a diplomatic manner, as far as we knew. Turkey did come in with us thankfully for all concerned. Unaccountable behaviour continued on a much lower key which gave the usual pleasures to the gossips, plus the fleet!

We revelled in the luxurious warmth with a perfect sea breeze to carry off excess heat. Our topees had special red linings and were the order of the day as the sun was really quite intense. Sunbathing was wisely forbidden.

Great excitement when someone with binoculars could see land, just a thick line that looked like a cloud on the horizon. During our daily session with Matron we were again warned about the various tropical diseases that were virulent in Freetown, especially malaria caused by the mosquitoes. When the ship became stationary off the port we were instructed to wear long white drill leggings and detachable long sleeves over our short sleeved uniform dresses as a safeguard against the aforesaid bugs.

Another surprise instruction from the hierarchy, with a somewhat limited imagination, was to give the troops a dance as they felt they had paid insufficient attention to their conditions on the lower decks. I should have thought they were pretty ghastly, with only a very narrow and limited deck space up above their waterline deck. They had been given permission to use a smaller deck for sleeping but not nearly large enough space for all of them to escape from their overcrowded sleeping quarters, literally the ship's hold.

The dance would be held when the ship became stationary off Freetown. Many details of this arrangement were left unsaid. We were all allocated to take part in this sweltering heat – whose crazy idea was this? Instructions were given to us to wear these cotton drill leggings that came up to our waists and long sleeved dresses. After sunset it would be torture for us and the mosquitoes would be laughing.

It was wonderful to see land again, all so tropical and exotic, palm trees predominating but many flowering shrubs. There were the brilliant Bougainvillaea of all shades, Oleander of course and many kinds of fruit. Through the glasses one could see the colourful people in their tribal costumes and the busyness in the port with many tenders speeding to and fro with the various supplies for the ships. They brought the fruits we had been starved of for so long and many other such luxuries.

The heat was colossal and we were very much missing the sea breezes. The brazen sun was such that the shade was sought eagerly by most. The ballet exercising was suspended too as heat stroke was on the menu.

Now this proposed dance we thought bizarre. The decision made by whomever was to entertain several hundred troops, allowing them one dance each – this anyway was the theory – all in a room with two small windows, after sunset. We were forty-five sisters and forty-five men were given one ticket each for one dance with the temperature in the hundreds!Anyone who knows the British Tommy will guess their capabilities of mucking up the system to their advantage and so there was a certain amount of barter for tickets. I know the first chap I danced with managed three dances and the queue on deck never seemed to reduce.

Three times I had to go down to change out of my sweat-soaked uniform but after the third change and having no more to change into I gave up and had yet another bath. We saw not a sign of either of the Matrons or the planners of this campaign!

After leaving Freetown we did not stop again until we saw the tip of that glorious Table Mountain, having taken six weeks to get there. Alas once again there was to be no landing here at Cape Town. We lay at least two miles off and longed to go ashore.

The whole scene was so clear. For two days the mountain had no cloud over it, what the locals call the tablecloth, which in a curious way pours over the flat top of the mountain and appears to drag down the sides as a tidy housewife would do.

Sadly we were moved on, around the corner as it were, to Durban. We were going into the Indian Ocean.

AFRICA

At last we were informed that our destination was Durban. This would take a day or so, nevertheless it would be lovely to be on terra firma once more, no doubt we should feel wobbly for a while and it would give understanding to the 'drunken sailor' theory.

As we approached Durban and at approximately a mile off every one became aware, very faintly at first, of a very beautiful voice singing and all fell silent, listening. The usual comments of mermaids on rocks calling to the sailors, of course, but as we got a little closer to the coast the singing obviously was real.

The wonderful voice of a lady. Getting closer still we made out a group of people awaiting our arrival. It was quite incredible. Evidently she was an opera singer, and being able to throw her voice a great distance across the sea, she met every convoy that came into Durban, until the end of the War.

After being given our instructions and told exactly when and how we should go ashore, most of us went on deck. It was so wonderful to see this exciting country of which we had only learnt about at school. Looking over the port, and preparing to dock all was efficiency, with a mixture of races all contributing to our landing.

We had said our 'good byes' to friends on board, some more affectionate than others and were loaded on to various cars transporting us through this, what was then, orderly though exotic town.

Five of us were taken to the luxurious Edward Hotel on the Promenade. It was elegant, with guests who were equally so. The hotel manager received us, escorting us to the dining room kindly saying he would be glad to help in any way. On asking from where in the UK had we come and discovering that I had come from Wales he declared he also was Welsh.

Looking around this very lovely dining room with

14

smart waiters in white tunic, trousers, turbans with red flashes, wearing white cotton gloves for serving food, was an unaccustomed luxury. At all the tables around the room what impressed us the most were large bowls of every kind of fruit, pineapple, grapes, oranges, none of which any of us had seen in many months. This was a veritable cornucopia, not having even seen an orange in a year.

Quite suddenly, we received orders allowing us to wear mufti, a great surprise. Hastily we made for the mouth-watering shops. To be able to buy without coupons was such a treat I bought a pink linen skirt with a navy blue shirt top, a rope of fine chunky beads exactly the same pink as the skirt and was happy with this simple purchase.

We had many invitations and were taken about by charming people who would come to the hotel to meet us. One particular lady with her ten-year-old daughter took us up to the Valley of a Thousand Hills and to Pietermaritzburg.

Having previously bought a five-year diary I was told it was disallowed so I decided to make a present of it to the young daughter. Neither were we permitted cameras of course; how I could do with the photographs now.

Invitations came from officers to go dancing as a party, where we wore our simple mufti. Later, on board, I was leaning over a ship's rail only to see my chunky necklace fall into the sea! heartbreaking.

Two wonderful weeks; then orders to pack and be ready to be collected at a certain time next day. Trying to thank the manager for his many kindnesses, we were collected and taken to the docks once more.

This time it was a smaller coastal vessel with no military, but several civilian gentlemen who had not had leave for a considerable time, and had taken this opportunity to get to Kenya. They were charming and friendly and we enjoyed their company and getting to know them was easier on a small boat. To while away the time we played party games as we did at home whenever any numbers came. So in the afternoons having been given permission by the Captain we even played 'hide and seek' all over the deck finding great places such as inside the huge coils of rope. Every one took part with lots of fun and laughter. After dinner we played Consequences and card games, with introductions to new ones, and always treasure hunts.

The boat sailed close to the coast, passing the Spice Islands, the scents of spices was prevalent, especially cloves. The Islands were so tropical and lovely, gorgeous beaches with turquoise seas. How we longed to visit

There were alarms when we learned that a Jap sub was tailing us, and we had to scramble into our lifejackets with our panic bags and sit at our stations quietly until danger had passed. This happened several times, reminding us of the object of the exercise.

This lovely trip took two weeks. Arriving in dock again, it was at dawn, the sky a pale blue streaked with pinks and deep orange as the sun had not yet come over the horizon and all was sleepy and quiet. There were a few Arabs and Africans rubbing their eyes all concerned with this ship arriving.

Remaining on board, as was usual, to see the naval officers who gave us our passports plus some local money, we said our 'good byes' sadly, to our travelling companions, and disembarked complete with both Matrons into a bus making for the only train of the day, leaving for Nairobi.

This was an adventure. The scents of the town of Mombassa with the several mixed races colourful bright and gay and strange languages of all these races. The Arabs I had thought previously were the more silent and detached. The African was a jolly fellow, very dark shining skin.

Boarding the train we were given a comfortable compartment with four bunks, this being an overnight journey. The heat was quite intense in the day. We were told the train would leave at four. After settling and checking our luggage we made for the dining car. No cooling systems in those days; glad in the acceptable English fashion; drank hot tea! The train carried all civilian passengers.

The ladies seemed to be residents of Nairobi and others lived out on farms. The men were bronzed looking, very masculine in their smart shorts while the ladies were still in their twenties and thirties fashions. However they were a little surprised at the influx of all these young women, although we behaved well. We were something from another world but I am sure on getting to know them they were charming.

The train was starting; every one was agog, having been told to look out for game and eventually the animals appeared silent as shadows on this vast veldt. Already the light was fading as we were now right on the Equator and darkness came like a curtain; just the head of a giraffe silhouetted against the last ray of light.

A most comfortable journey overnight to the rhythm of the train. Waking at dawn to see the incredible sight of Kilamenjaro some twenty thousand feet in the blue sky covered in snow, not unlike a Christmas pud with white sauce. This on the equator, surely one of God's jokes, or to show us the power of nature.

We saw several zebra and kudu amongst the gazelle that was such a thrill and most exciting for us. We gathered at the carriage windows as long as possible.

Arriving in Nairobi we found a small town, by English standards, the main streets wide and very colourful, with the delicate blue of the jacaranda trees just dropping their petals covering the ground into a blue haze; the brilliant wine red of the bougainvillea arched to the ground in contrast, of colour, joined in then with a different blue of the plumbago in flower down the centre of these long thoroughfares; it was striking,

Then we were transported some miles out of the town to a hospital that had previously been a large stable block for racehorses and their jockeys. It now accommodated African troops needing hospitalising.

For the first time we were in native Africa surrounded by bright brick red earth which many people who are familiar with that region will vividly remember. Our accommodation was in long huts where the African jockeys had been housed for the racing. They had boarded floors unlike the wards which were earthen. Our bedrolls were brought to us in the huts and our rooms soon stank to high heaven with the damp as they had been in the holds of the ships since we had left the UK. Brown paper was issued in order to cover our wet mattresses also some dry sheets with the result the whole night was spent in the crackling of paper with every one turning and twisting in utter discomfort.

We were all up before dawn as we were unable to rest and had to get ready for instructions and probably work. But first of all there were the smelly wet beds to deal with. At sun up we hauled the offending articles out into the sunshine with frequent turning. Nairobi is up at 6,000ft but the sun was very hot in the afternoons and cooled down agreeably in the evening.

My first job was to assist two sisters with a ward of seventy mental breakdown cases. They were raw recruits; never been outside their native villages; full of enthusiasm to fight for, as they thought Kingy Georgy. Sadly they were very primitive and modern life was out of their scope and a shattering experience.

Today it's hard to understand this as television has broken down so many barriers into modern life. The effect then on them was alarming. The seventy patients, some like zombies, unable to accept what they were doing; others huge powerful men, five of whom were in straight jackets, fixed to the beds. My instructions were to give morphia injections to most three times daily to maintain order and relax them. One English psychiatrist investigated each case and endeavoured to assess the extent of their mental derangement. The saddest thing was when they tried to communicate by calling us 'Mamma'. They were just children

One day a patient disappeared up a very tall tree, refusing to come down. All the African orderlies tried their best. Finally the authorities were advised to send for his bibbi (wife) from his village some miles away to come and talk to him. He was up there in his pyjamas with all kinds of possibilities, but refused to move. It took several days; no doubt he got hungry.

On our off duty we naturally investigated the town shops and restaurants, having many invitations to lunch in parties and racing back to get on duty. Some fun dances in the nice hotels and on the whole we had a good time. I am sure we awoke Nairobi, always in our distinctive uniform with the exception of dances, until permission was given for mufti.

My next move was to the Leprosy ward. Knowing nothing of tropical diseases I was amazed by the extremely cheerful atmosphere. In any case it did not take much to make the African laugh as they were full of fun and, like children were easily amused.

The head orderly was an African sergeant called John who was a Christian convert, very cheerful with a big smile and the Bible under his arm coming on duty. I had just come on duty and as routine should have received the keys of the poison cupboard from the sister I was replacing but instead John had them and I retrieved them from him. This was irregular. It seemed that the previous sister had put a great deal of trust in John. To my astonishment the Military Police appeared in the afternoon and asked to see the keys of the poison cupboard and to check the contents. They interviewed John and I tried to explain I had only been on the ward a few hours and could they tell me what was going on. They had to arrest John who had been practising a private medical clinic in the bazaar and had given someone an overdose and the man had died. It was most unfair to me as I had only been on duty an hour, but because I was on duty at the time of the arrest I was responsible. This would be a civil court case.

We had many things to learn about nursing, the natives and their wonderful country and also the language. We remained as a unit, giving the previous staff a chance of leave. We did not know it of course, but the whole unit was intended for the Far East eventually, Burma. The grand plan had been to train up the Kenyan plus the Chinianga troops from Southern Rhodesia, who were good trackers in the forests to fight in the forests of Burma. In due course the nursing was also planned to this end, selecting a certain number of other staff who were Rhodesian and therefore spoke the language of their troops.

There was another incident that was an experience. A tremendous army of soldier ants marched with their colony through our sleeping quarters completely covering the walls, beds, and every nook and cranny while we stood from a distance and watched. This took about two hours. We gazed with fascination and were told it was most dangerous to go near as the huge soldier ants could kill anyone who interfered.

In due course I was sent to Tanganyika to replace a Rhodesian sister from a small station in Moshi which was truly Africa, a few hundred miles by train. I took a sad farewell to my friends especially as no one knew what was happening. Security was so bad in Kenya that it was well known that anyone could find out the movement of troops in the bazaar from the Arabs, at a price!

I had to leave the train at Arusha and was met by a truck with an African driver at Voi and taken to Moshi, driving over red earth roads on the edge of tropical forest, which the driver told me was the home of many elephant.

I suspected the reason for the nine sisters left in Africa and me, coincided with a slight altercation I once had with Matron regarding my hair, it was short, but she would prefer an 'Eton crop,' It was hidden under my uniform cap in any case; we shall never quite know.

I was made welcome by the elderly matron and eventually the four other sisters in the small wooden cottage. I had a little room with a magnificent view of Kilimenjaro, right up to the snows and skies beyond.

There was just a short walk up to the hospital where I was given a ward of British soldiers, for these were the troops assembling for Burma; but of course we knew nothing about that at the time

The orderlies were well trained Africans and to my astonishment were permitted by the ward doctor to take blood from a vein! Their knowledge of anatomy was due to their close association with their animals on their shambas (farms). They were very accurate, far better than the doctors, who recognised this.

Our social life revolved round the officers who were such fun and such gentlemen. We had picnics. They would call in to the mess and have coffee with whoever was there, as we all had varying duty times. They arranged to take us on night walks through the forest to see different animals, such as one time to watch the hippos in the river when we had to be very quiet in case they came out of the river as they could be dangerous. Someone found out my birthday was due and planned a moonlight picnic above the tree line on a plateau looking up under Kilomenjaro snows. The men were mostly Rhodesian or English who had adopted Africa years earlier and knew the dangers.

John, a very charming man called for me in the morning to take me shopping in the bazaar to buy everything for the evening party, chickens etc. which were given to the cook plus instructions about cakes and puds. It was evidently possible to take a car as far as the site. With several cars in convoy they took us all. It was a full moon, very romantic, and someone had brought a windup gramophone and it was a great party, the best ever. There is always a sad sequel, John was killed in Burma some time later, such a waste of a good man.

Another time I happened to meet a couple of the Fleet Air Arm Officers who were so pleasant. They asked us to the mess and asked me whether I would like to take a flip in the plane, which of course I gladly accepted. But first of all both the pilot and I had to sign a typed note which proclaimed that, 'We the undersigned hereby certify that we absolve the Royal Navy of all responsibility for any injury or death which may result from our being carried in a Royal Navy Naval Aircraft. We certify that the flight is undertaken entirely at our own risk and that neither we, our dependants or heirs will have any claim whatsoever on HM Navy, the Pilot of the aircraft and/or crew in the case of any injury or death resulting from the flight.' The piece of paper is still in my possession.

Up and away we went in a Swordfish which has two cockpits with open tops the back seat being the pilot's seat. My pilot flew us quite low over the hospital, so much so that the Africans were dancing about calling 'ndegi, ndegi' (bird) and recognising me called out 'Memsahib' and caused great excitement. Needless to say the hospital authorities complained, stopping further flights!

In the meantime I was being interrupted with requests to go back to Nairobi to give evidence for the wretched court case which was so unfair. My return meant I had to leave the train at one or two in the morning and somone would meet me. Sometimes the Chaplin of the Brigade would offer to do this, putting a camp bed in the back of the truck. But the last thing I wanted to do was sleep as coming through Savo was real lion country and so exciting seeing them like great green-yellow head lamps of eyes by the hundreds all around with the smells of Africa cooling down after the intense heat of the day.

I was once taken for the weekend to stay with some delighful English people who owned a sugar plantation. It was so beautiful and luxurious; lovely rooms with antique furniture and a handsome house and location, at dinner a slow beating of the drums would begin in the native compound making a perfect background and harmony.

Recently I spent four months in South Africa only to find it quite turned on its head; desperately sad for Africa and the African. They are trying to run before they can walk.

Having had to visit Nairobi for the court case yet again, the powers that be decided to send me to Nairobi until the case ended which left me broken hearted. But something else over shadowed this, which was a thousand times worse. The officers in Moshi broke the news to me but had withheld it for a little while, out of kindness to me.

I knew all my unit that I had left in Nairobi had sailed for Ceylon and I imagined they had gone on to India. Alas they were one day off Ceylon and were torpedoed. Two thousand women were aboard, the forty-five sisters of my unit and the rest were Wrens, ATS, and Waafs. They were in the centre of the convoy well protected, most were down to lunch and three only were saved, as they were on deck. Being hit by four torpedoes the ship sank in about three minutes.

The saved were the two nursing sisters I knew, one the sister I had replaced in Moshi who was a Rhodesian, the other Guys Hospital trained who was also a sister, having come out with us from the UK. These two were phenominal athletes. The third person was a naval officer. No one else I was told was saved. This was kept most secret, and I do not know who did spill the beans four months later.

Having failed to get any details I finally found the ship was the Knedive Ismail troopship sunk on the 12th of February 1944. This information I found fifty years later in a bookshop that dealt in the history of both wars. Of all places it was in the seaside town of Ventnor in the Isle of Wight where I now live. To my horror the information disclosed that the Knedive was carrying munitions in the hold.

It was so easy to get into hot water in the army it seemed. In my off duty one morning I was walking to the Baazar before the sun became too hot and a sergeant on a motor bike pulled up and offered me a lift. I did question it, but he assured me it would be all right, as there was no one about and I felt it would be churlish to refuse, and got on the pillion. We had a speedy run in, rushing through the early morning air and it was wonderful, but can you believe it? He was reported to the Brigadier and in his defence said, 'It was worth it Sir!' I think it became a bit of a joke in the end; what a fuss about nothing.

Leaving Moshi was a great sadness to me. I loved it all and was angry of course at the stupid reason for my going. Being a moderately law abiding person I could not understand this unhappy move. I had had one experiance in the court and given my evidence, for what it was worth. I arrived in Nairobi and found a few friends still there. Information reached me that the court case had been settled; what a game!

My next posting was to Somalia. There was a weekly train as far as Isiolo, meeting up with a convoy of trucks the other side of Mount Kenya. No other information was offered. I had a whole week to fill in. My friends arranged a farewell luncheon at the hotel with several chaps of the army. My train was leaving at two thirty and someone noticed the hotel clock had stopped and we had five minutes to get to the station.

Crisis. The chaps were all action; one went for my luggage; we dashed for the cars; someone paid the bill; four cars exceeded all the speed limits and simply tore through the town, arriving at the station as the whistle blew and I was lifted into the last coach as it was moving; my luggage on the train somewhere!

When I managed to recover, and found the compartment reserved, I met a fairly large lady who, unbeknown to me was the new Matron to Somalia and was to be my travelling companion! 'Crikey! What a good start, how do I begin to apologise?' 'You have had a whole week to prepare for this journey' etc. which of course was true. The truth sounded a dead duck. My new Matron on the whole accepted my very weak explanation. I received no sympathy, but she was fairly dubious about me for a while, not the best start of a six-month tour.

At the end of our train journey we were met by a truck, just the two of us and taken to Isiolo where we met up with the convoy of ten trucks. The Transport Officer was so nice, and surprised to find a corporal in charge of the convoy, but evidently he was very experienced, receiving his third stripe on the journey. He was not only to be in charge of all the trucks and drivers but I was to be his passenger in a fifteen-hundredweight. He was very quiet but I was to discover he had a lovely sense of cockney humour.

As a new venture the Italian prisoners were let out of prison, being permitted to drive the trucks, which delighted them. First stop Mogadishu where earlier Mussolini had invaded, leaving many Italians who were now under British command.

Mount Kenya looked wonderful as we gazed from the back. Neither Matron nor I had seen it before. It was such a contrast from Kilimajaro. We made the most of it, as next morning at dawn we should be moving.

My personal servant, whom I had had since my arrival in the country, was with me. He was very good in his slow African way and loyal. He put up my camp bed where I wanted it under a thorn tree from which my mosquito net could be hung. He brought me early morning tea and on the journey collected my meals. He was called Karioki.

The journey was intended to take six days to Mogadishu. The trucks were all lined up with my truck leading, with Matron in the middle in a much larger truck. There was such a mixture of races, several officers, the highest rank was a major, some captains, 2nd lieutenants and other ranks, African Indian troops. These were all passengers.

Finding the corporal I put my luggage in the back of his truck and prepared with the rest to follow him. Thankfully I was in the leading vehicle as looking back along the trucks I could see they were all engulfed in smothering red dust.

After an hour's travelling my driver chose to stop to check that the lorries were all keeping up; due to the dust we were unable to count them while moving. This being doubtful corporal decided to run the length of the convoy as we seemed to have only nine. Turning around then to go and look for the stray we found him five miles back.

In his eagerness to please he had taken a number of pieces of engine apart, laying them on the road, trying to find a fault. I heard a few expressive cockney words and 'Corp' got it all together again. We started once more, catching and joining up with the rest. It was explained that to stop was dangerous, as left behind no one could guarantee safety. He would be in mortal danger without water. 'Hoot loudly but no mechanics' he was told.

The order was to stop earlier the first day to get accustomed to setting up camp, getting nets put up and well tucked under the mattress to fend off over-friendly snakes and mosquitoes before the little devils got going. Here they could be monstrous

Our evening meal was bully beef stew with Army biscuits two inches square by a quarter of an inch thick, as hard as iron. Matron and I would join some of the company for the meal just into the scrub trees on the road side, when some of the 'wags' would try to scare me about the animals around about us, as we sat around the fire

Creeping under my net I was content to sleep looking at the moon. The sun dropping with such suddenness it became instantly dark, showing the millions of stars in their pure brilliance. Without lights and in velvet black darkness it was an experience of a lifetime.

Being sensible Matron had her camp bed in the back of a large truck, quite near. Suddenly I was awake hearing deep-throated rumbling sounds accompanied by the echoing roar of a lion. It sounded as though it was at my bed head, its echo was penetrating, reaching the ends of the earth. Hastily I scrambled my bed into the back of the truck.

We were awakened at five am with a cup of tea, very smoky and sweet. I had a splash in the canvas basin and jumped into trousers, now uniform equipment, and was ready by six o'clock. My corporal was inspecting the drivers and trucks with the Personel Officer, both gave me a smile enquring kindly about the night.

We drove for three hours then stopped for breakfast, my boy bringing me a fried egg with bread and tea. We all had our water bottles filled, as the heat in the afternoons was extreme. The country was changing into thorn trees as far as the eye could see. Their thorns were three to four inches long and fierce. Apparently the natives used them for sewing. Everyone took exercise and we ladies tried to be discreet over spending pennies, it was difficult. Having been warned not to penetrate more than so many yards into the scrub as it was very easy to get lost and lose direction and the road entirely.

Once or twice the corporal had to have emergency runs checking on the trucks. As they weren't always in order continual checking was somewhat exhausting in the afternoons.

We were now on our way to Wajir where we would stop for our lunch and a break. It is a walled city thousands of years old, with life unchanged since BC, with the exception of one solitary German doctor who had made his life there serving the people. He had trained a native girl to assist him.

Matron and I went and introduced ourselves and were shown around the little operating theatre and anteroom. In spite of the earthen floors it was very clean and orderly. His nurse had beautifull dark skin and Egyptian features, high cheekbones, narrow unsmiling face and slim figure. The white uniform and head veil and coffee coloured skin would have made a stunning painting. The two rooms were mud and wattle with earthen floors.

By this time we had quite a following of local inhabitants. As the interpreter explained, we were the first white women they had ever seen. Matron decided we should visit the bazaar, the few duckers ('shops') and purchase some small thing.

The crowd increased; some of the young girls were feeling my arm not believing the colour, which was really a very natural thing to do. Karioki was behind me. Making a way through the crowd we smiled and waved goodbye. The water we replenished at times was very brackish and undrinkable so we used it for washing.

I was always so impressed with the District Commissioners of the Colonial Service who kept the peace over these thousands of miles of territories for years, negotiating with the local headmen of the villages in a democratic manner, understanding and regarding the ethics of all their communities. I am afraid I got very hot under the collar when later the Americans were eager to criticise the Colonial Service.

The personnel officer we got to know as Bill had heard from headquarters that the whole convoy should go no further as the rains had broken up country. This could flood the country for miles around. Jo, my corporal got through to command to someone else in HQ who was senior and insisted we went on. The heat was so intense in the afternoons, before the rains. It built up and the relief then when the rains broke was enormous, but now we would be in trouble if we were caught.

We decided there were too many brass hats in Nairobi with great lack of communication, very little consideration and no personal experience of this journey. On we went and hadn't gone far when an army sergeant stopped us. He was standing in the middle of the road waving his arms. He *was* glad to see us. His truck was in the bush off the road with three Askaries one of whom had tried to light a fire with an old Italian hand grenade he had found; being alive it had blown off his hand.

There was a discussion and the decision was made for Corporal and I to take the injured man back to Wajir to the doctor and leave him there to recover. So we made room for him in the back of the truck, driving back some ten miles or more. We met up again with the doctor and it needed very little explanation. He took one look and understood. There we left our patient in good hands, arranging to have him back to his unit when fully recovered.

We had no food, but water of course, and hoped we didn't break down. By this time it was getting late and had been dark for some hours. It was midnight when we returned and everyone was asleep. I was too tired to eat but Karioki, bless him met me with tea and Matron was kind.

In the morning I awoke to a chorus of loud voices. I had been allowed to sleep late, making up for my previous tiring day, but missing much of the excitement as the Sergeant Major had been robbed. It was so difficult to keep a straight face when only the day before he had warned us, telling every one how to protect their clothes and money when sleeping outside.

The Somalis were notorious thieves; they were like shadows. On this journey they appeared suddenly to be there, standing motionless. Their ability to stand very still on one leg for so long was fascinating, with a stick called a kobogo across their shoulders held up in their hands. This was a familiar pose. Short dark men, usually in spotless turban and lungi swathed around to below their knees. Usually one lonely man, but rarely no more than two silently watching. No one ever saw them arrive or leave but suddenly you looked and they weren't there. Without a sound. Quite eerie.

They had removed the Sergeant Major's uniform from under his pillow, which contained his money and even his sheet from underneath him and under the mosquito net, quite a feat. Someone who knew explained how it was done. Blowing in the ear got the chap to turn over. I wonder. I did learn that the biggest danger was to wake up, then you would be no more. I'm afraid I was to learn this when living there.

Next day Matron called me to her truck asking me to inspect the British troops who had suspected an infectious rash that they thought was measles. I found the rash and a low temperature, but no measles, thank heavens. We just had to watch, wait and see. The Italian driver was most helpful offering 'pot permang' to bathe the rash. What a thing an outbreak of measles would be here! It wasn't until years later when reading David Niven's The *Moon's a Balloon* did I realise why the Italian was carrying pot permang!

My next anxiety was Matron. She was exhausted. I found her crying a lot and we talked together. I tried to persuade her to stay in her camp bed while travelling but to no avail. She was proud and hated to give in. With the heat

28

so intense we had to stop driving in the afternoons, giving every one a rest. Four of us played some awful Bridge with Matron and Bill and another to keep our sanity, it was hysterically funny, but good for us.

I took to visiting the trucks and altogether we had picked up twenty other trucks that had got into trouble and tagged on to us. If only we could have a bath! We had spent five days by now and should already have been in Mogadishu.

We heard a rumble in the distance. I said to Jo 'look at the horizon, there's a heat haze so thick that I can't see the road.' He pulled up and getting out said that it was no heat haze but water as far as the eye could see and flooding far and wide. This was the start of the cascade from up country thousands of miles away. This could compare with the cascade that comes down dry riverbeds building up to a height of seven or eight feet in narrow beds called a bore. Here it was spreading over flatter country, now soaking like blotting paper making the road impassable.

Jo and I had made so many trips up and down the trucks rescuing and keeping them together. Food and water were becoming difficult, but now I would have a bathe. Getting into my costume I had my dip before the truck drivers came to view the water. Goodness knows what was being carried down with the fast flowing current. This had come from the Juba River. It flowed so fast that it took Matron's precious soap that she had loaned me. I was so cross with myself but the current was so much faster than I anticipated and I had to cling on. She was not very pleased.

Now of course senior ranks, a Major and a Captain, who were passengers, decided to deal with the emergency in a very unpleasant manner, taking our personal bottles of water and pooling all and allotting one cup per day. Bill being personnel manager tried to explain the orthodox method for such an emergency but they pulled rank on him and became officious.

Jo maintained, in a positive and quiet way, that the trucks were his responsibility and he would wait a day allowing the water to soak into the ground. He arranged to organise chains for next morning, stuffed the exhausts with waterproof material and trucks were towed through the water two by two, trusting no water would get in. His wonderful humourous remarks saved the day for me. My contribution was that I did not like the Captain's fancy suede shoes!

Great cheering was given to the first two trucks through the flood. Many congratulations to the Sergeant [now] and it couldn't have come at a better time.

The African boys were gathering wood for the fires when they came across a black scorpion as large as a dinner plate. They brought it in for all to see, having killed it of course. The thick curling tail was eight inches long and the granddaddy of all the old African ethics was that dead creatures were the safest

By the second afternoon they were gradually getting trucks over, but fearful of getting stuck all the time. There would be no roads left now. Some of us played crazy Bridge again with lots of laughter, just a reaction to our predicament. With unfair criticisms and crass authority from the Captain and aloof Major. I never liked his shoes!.

We all longed to be moving, simply to get the air moving around us. Mysterious Somalis watched like phantoms, silently. Suddenly one just noticed them, looking again, they had gone not the snap of a twig, or a leaf moved. They knew how to cross the flood, the dense bush was no problem, they could read it like a map... they knew each bush.

On the third and last day, after some recognisance, it was decided to make a detour around the huge lake through the bush. There were five or six vehicles remaining and we had the dubious pleasure of leading them through the unknown bush. We should all have been too low in the water. An ominous silence fell as Sergeant, and I set off and in order to circumvent the water we had to charge through the bush.There were no roads, just crashing through the fierce thorns on either side, it being so hot we had to have the windows open. To escape the thorns that were crowding into the cabin I had to hide under the dashboard. Sergeant had a terrible time as he was dodging tree trunks, driving in low gear as best he could in the rough ground with difficult angles. How he found his way was nothing short of a miracle, and this went on for most of the day. Finally we saw the road once more and the trucks and every one waiting anxiously, Matron especially. However all the trucks were together. My goodness that was some experience. Now we seemed to have forty trucks!

Next morning I was left to sleep on, awakening at seven o'clock to most awful and extraordinary quietness. Dressing hurriedly I found a very unusual scene. Matron was sitting quietly having her breakfast at her camp table while two embarrassed private soldiers were standing fairly near. The trucks were all lined up with the little Major glaring at us, arms folded, holding his officer authoritative stick. Matron insisted I should join her and have my breakfast and ignore everything. I made an attempt to eat while asking what was going on. Evidently she had been put under 'close arrest' for disobeying his order which was that the convoy should be made ready to start at four am in order to make up for lost time.

She had insisted that I was exhausted and I was to be allowed my rest! What a mess, a bizarre scene if ever there was one. I was trying to hurry but she insisted I took my time. She was icy calm and quite deliberate. It was most enormously kind of her on my account but an absurd sketch; in the middle of the bush no one could possibly go anywhere!

The Major kept up this farce for the rest of the journey. It was such a relief to get into our fifteen hundredweight away from all that and enjoy the wonderful cockney humour once again.

Again we stopped for meals along another ancient walled city and for exercise walked and purchased from the 'duckas'. Again they had not seen white women. On the way I several times saw the most beautiful young girls with Egyptian features. One particularly I shall always remember with a pitcher of water on her head; such carriage and poise, so very beautiful.

Now we had only a couple of hundred miles to the tarmac road and Mogadishu. That would bring this part of the journey to ten days. Only twenty-four hours there and off to Hargeysa which was another week in a truck.

We continued our routine of running up and down the

convoy checking that everyone was there; forty trucks, all thankful to be with us, and as we landed on tarmac every one cheered. As a result of lack of water in the heat I developed cystitis and apart from being very uncomfortable I had the awful embarrassing need to stop frequently and find a bush. Sergeant was so understanding and good, saying the Aficans loved the excuse to do the same.

Our arrival in the town was so great. Now we could soak in a bath, change into clean clothes and enjoy an Italian meal, sleep in a proper bed and enjoy a few civilised hours.

I spent quite some time trying to contact the Air Force and succeeded, off the record, in getting a seat on the little aeroplane taking but only a few hours to get to Hargeysa. This was for Matron. Proud of my achievement I broke the news to Matron who flatly refused to take it.

Having the morning free was bliss. A great number of Italians remained in the town all fully employed by the British. There were good restaurants and cafés; to me it seemed heaven.

We met the convoy once more and our friends, starting off on a five-day journey with good roads and no fear of floods. This proved to be a normal journey with regular stops and fewer vehicles and very nice Colonial Service passengers.

Hargeysa was a tented area mostly Army. The only building was the hospital and the sisters' Mess, all mud and wattle; concrete floors, thankfully. There was some sort of concert or entertainment area where members of ENSA nobly came to entertain the troops and the ladies were put up at our Mess. Altogether it was a miserable place, but the actresses were a welcome diversion from the sisters at the Mess.

My first ward was of forty beds, all plaster cases; poor things mostly fully encased; they were of mixed races and some British. Italian orderlies were good and quite speedy.

Looking around my office I was horrified to see bugs crawling up the walls. Worse than that I discovered the bugs were in all the plasters and the patients were scratching continuously. What was wrong with everyone to overlook this? It was shocking.

I talked to the very nice senior doctor who was from middle Europe and very approachable, and in spite of that seemed to get very little response from the staff. We came to the conclusion that the entire ward should be washed down with disinfectant and all plasters renewed and my office to be whitewashed. The whole atmosphere was depressing, and generally the people were simply marking time until their six months was up to get back to Kenya

The countryside was quite wild. Packs of Hyena wandered at night, their cries and calls were so loud around us, scorpions everywhere, porcupines, huge turtles that could have been ridden, vermin of every kind. Most paths were thick with shed porcupine needles.

I had to acquire a dog for personal protection to keep in my room at night. As I have said before, the fact was that Somalis were dangerous thieves and were known to attack while you were asleep and in spite of locked doors would get in and if disturbed you could be stabbed. But their religious laws forbade them to touch, or be touched by a dog. He was a sweet puppy and a good companion.

There was a bazaar and Karioki always accompanied me. Dress materials were good and I enjoyed making clothes. My other occupation was creating a garden around the ward.

One time while at the bazaar, Karioki's money was stolen out of his pocket. He was so angry and called them really bad people and much more. I did what anyone would do by replacing his loss and he was pathetically grateful.

There was an open drain which if nothing else should be hidden, and to repeat what I had done in Moshi I grew zinnias which put the size of the Chelsea Flower Show displays to shame.

The butterflies were so beautiful as were the birds, a naturalist's paradise but no reference books available for either.

For a break we were given a lift into Berbera, an even hotter place on the rugged coast across the waters of the Indian Ocean from Aden. Three of the sisters came. There we met some pleasant officers. We were mutually glad of each other's company. They took us down to the seashore where we all dug up oysters of enormous size, discovering later that it was an old burial ground!

The Somalis were a mean people, mostly nomadic. The British maintained them by bringing ten large trucks of food from Kenya each week They moved to different places with fifty or sixty camels, the women walking with babies while the men rode. They must have covered thousands of miles.

On night duty we took umbrellas, not for the rain but to protect our heads from stones which were hurled at us when walking between the wards.

What was known as the short rains came before I left. It came in the form of a seven-foot bore, literally coming down the dry riverbed standing that high. One unfortunate British officer had the nasty experience of being held down in the river by a couple of Somalis who tried to drown him. Fortunately someone rescued him.

On another little break we visited another Mess in Dera towards Abyssinia. There was an acute hairpin bend and as we had to go very slowly children overwhelmed the car pouring all sorts of fruits into our laps for money. This was my first acquaintance with custard apples, a soft green, the size of an apple and full of large black seeds.

As a final piece of information, I did meet a Somali patient, highly intelligent, who had blue eyes, spoke Welsh fluently, and had been brought up in Cardiff, South Wales before the war.

This was the end of my six months. Now back to Kenya, and then what?

Return to Kenya from Somalia

My farewells said, a new experience over. I decided it was a complex place in which to live and work. Sad parting with my dog to a friend. Karioki given leave to go to his village.

A straight run this time of five days, with only one interesting item of running into a swarm of locusts so immense that they literally blocked out the sun; having to use headlamps. This was a swarm of multi-millions, taking five hours to pass through, very slowly. We had to stop frequently to wash the windscreens and bonnets of the wagons, thus giving the Africans an opportunity to catch handfuls as they made good eating, so we were told, very like prawns it was said. I always thought this might make a good commercial enterprise as the locusts were feeding on their corn and wheat. The road was littered with hundreds of squashed pink bodies making the rough road a little slippery but what a tarmac road would be like I dread to think.

On arriving at Nyeri, which was a green and pleasant place, such a contrast to Somalia. The Mess was comfortable with cheerful chintzes, good food and all so well run by a local lady, Mrs Brown. There was a well loved Outspan Hotel, a flawless golf course, good fairways and trees which I had missed so much, a fine place to live.

Many very wealthy people had houses there, also on the coast, with holidays in UK. Their war effort was entertaining the Army for weekend house parties, always the men. One of the invited guests told me that the ratio of officers and other ranks was very indiscriminate, at such times a general could be placed next to a private soldier at these lavish dinners which was embarrassing for both for a weekend. Entertainment at private parties in hotels would include about thirty officers with just two of these wealthy ladies dancing in turns with the officers. None of the young ladies of the services were ever asked. The hostesses were middle aged.

It was a very English way of life as the climate was ideal, being up at eight thousand feet, the afternoons were fairly hot.

Karioki returned from his village with a most handsome cockerel under his arm. Walking through the compound as his contemporaries made admiring comments he presented this magnificent bird to me with great aplomb. Trying hard not to be surprised but delighted at the same time, I thanked him very much with my mind busy wondering what am I going to do with it! I gave him some money and he seemed happy.

Taking the bird up to the Mess I found Mrs Brown who came to my rescue by putting him in the hen coup. Some weeks later I happened to be passing the larder and a large plucked bird was hanging up, I did not go into lunch that day.

I was working on an 'other ranks' ward, plus a small ward for Officers with what 17th century writers called 'the clap', various kinds of venereal diseases.

Later on I worked on a tuberculosis ward for Africans having had some year and half training on this in civilian life. I was very concerned with the Africans' highly infectious and dangerous habit of spitting on the ground when outside. Mentioning this to the Consultant I asked him what we could do about it, he simply said 'Oh that's all right it will simply dry up and blow away'. This doctor was the son-in-law of Sir Phillip Manson Barr the man I was later to study under at the Tropical Diseases Hospital in London.

When I could get transport I would go to the Outspan Hotel and walk around the beautiful grounds where on one occasion I met Lady Baden Powell who with Lord Baden Powell had a cottage at the hotel. She explained they spent some time here each year.

After some months, we all moved again, this time to the coast for another voyage. Mombassa was very hot and sticky. There was a large hospital. Tropical beaches, coconut palms, glorious flowering trees, banks of flowering shrubs, colour every where; sand so burning hot that by ten o'clock it was too hot to go bare foot.

INDIA

I was joined once more by several sisters, introducing each other at the reporting office of Mombasa and we embarked on yet another troopship. This was an old converted pleasure cruiser still with the same stewards for the cabins, each now having several bunks, in spite of which we were politely asked, 'May I run your bath Ma'am?' which was so gracious. The iron baths with the mahogany surrounds held the old standards.

As the tide of war was changing, the Japanese were no longer in evidence in the Indian Ocean. We had five peaceful days before arriving in Colombo Harbour, Ceylon, another exotic harbour of the sub-continent.

This was altogether a different atmosphere from Africa. The people were better-educated and mature with thousands of years of culture and knowledge of the arts, crafts and Civic Administration.

They were mostly short and wiry with smaller refined features and jet-black glossy hair. Ladies and girls of the richer class had delightful manners; shyness but with a quiet refinement and confidence, wearing lovely silk saris which added to their grace. The race as a whole was quicker witted which would have surprised the dear African.

For our temporary stay we were given rooms in the old hospital staff accommodation. I was soon made aware that the local snakes enjoyed the dripping showers in the bathrooms. I had no hesitation in calling one of the boys to inspect that department before use.

The scenery was tropical and beautiful with extensive beaches. Shopping was a joy with the whole atmosphere happy and fun. Luncheon at the Galle Face Hotel was a treat. It was frequented by the local rich and sophisticated plus a number of British Army and Navy Service people. We met up with some of these who asked three of us to

The Author in army tropical uniform

The Author with her children in Kenya, January 1953

Nanny at Subukia during Mau Mau

Our gardener at Subukia

Shufarama, Anuradhapura Ceylon

Tea picking in India

Donald feeding the birds at 'our' lake Isle of Wight

Canada geese and young

supper and dance at the 'Silver Fawn' where we enjoyed an excellent dinner and dancing. Later I heard some wag had called it the 'Septic Prawn'.

What a civilised place to live I thought then, how sad now, so many places in turmoil. The British were responsible for all these countries where I worked. Africa, India and Ceylon were especially peaceful and now many of their citizens are at war with each other.

Ten days of this life was too short. Soon we were leaving for India, going by train, passing through great forests in the north of the island where the Tamils are causing such fighting now. The first night on the train continuing through to more exotic country and Madras. How we should have liked to stay and gone up to those hills, the Nilgiries and tea plantations; but only one morning there.

Onward then to Hyderabad through many villages to Bombay. Here we waited a day, snatching a look at the *'Gateway to India'*, a great arch built when the Taj Mahal Hotel was built. This was a tragedy for the architect who made the mistake of building the hotel the wrong way round, sadly committing suicide, as he could not live with the disgrace.

Taking the train to the hill station of Poona there was all the usual excitement on the station; porters carrying such loads of luggage; everyone shouting to each other trying to find their compartment. Finally puffing along and in a few hours we arrived.

A truck awaited us and our luggage, sweeping us through torrential rain, dumping us in some outlandish place; wet and cheerless huts. Three days later we moved again to the 126th Military Hospital outside Poona and I was thankful. Two of us were to share a nice bungalow with a garden, a gardener and two bearers to clean and for our modest needs.

This was but a short distance from the vast hospital and I was confronted with having to ride a bicycle, which I had never learnt. Faced with this I simply had to grit my teeth and get on with it. One sister also had this problem but decided she would not ride but do the walking.

It was lunchtime and I was ushered into a very large dining room with the longest dining table I had ever seen, completely filled but for one empty place, with the highest-ranking Nursing Officers of the British Army. Never before had I seen such an assembly, a blinding display of red and gold flashes on so many shoulders. Being directed to the empty place I sat down; my neighbour, a mere Colonel, kindly smiled, making me feel easier. Looking vaguely around I simply replied when spoken to, trying not to be awe-struck, too overwhelmed to notice my food and finishing quickly as they were waiting for me, showing their good breeding, that we may rise together.

I was suffering greatly from my attempts at the art of riding my bike, leaving many impressions in the soft earth of the flowerbeds, apologising to the long-suffering gardener and in the end daring to go to Poona. With all the hazards India presents on its roads I successfully avoided cows, pigs, chickens and worst of all other cyclists and pedestrians. Motorists simply blew their horns until the cacophony was ignored; absolutely no idea of road rules, as there appeared to be none.

Now in all India there was high fever to 'Get Britain Out', like instant coffee it meant NOW.

Lord Mountbatten with his entourage equally so with a directive from the Labour Government who could not get rid of this Prime Socialist hot potato fast enough, pressurising for a speedy conclusion.

They were negotiating with Nehru and the most difficult and complicated character, Jinha, by his determination to split the Moslems from the Hindu, with the hideous result of mass murder of a people who had for hundreds of years lived peacefully together. The extent of politicians' megalomania knows no bounds, especially in a volatile people.

A few of the sisters were invited to ride the horses of the officers of the Poona and Bombay Hunt under the strict supervision of the Sergeant Major in charge. In order to get there we had to cycle several miles through highly inflammable meetings where Mr Gandhi was attracting thousands of cinder-dry people. Fortunately Mr Gandhi was a man of peace which gave me some confidence.

Surviving that excitement we presented ourselves correctly turned out for inspection in jodpurs etc., the S.M.

treated us like new recruits, concealing his enjoyment, but we were not fooled. The horses behaved like circus animals, instantly obeying his commands, giving us no time to 'collect'. This frequently found some of us on the ground, with S.M. roaring, 'Who the b..... h... gave you permission to dismount?' It was made known to us indirectly that a small sum was advised for this dubious pleasure considering it as 'backsheesh' for the S.M. This continued until it became 'too hot for the horses'. It was great fun and a diversion; besides the Irish weren't slow in giving him back as much as we received.

At this time I was doing night duty on a native ward for women. There I encountered the local animal wildlife that came out of the drains at night. The trouble started as soon as I came on duty it seemed, giving me time to go around the ward to talk with the patients and ayas who waited on them. First would come the bandicoots pushing their way through the quite heavy doors. They were larger than rabbits with an extra hump on the back of their necks. They could easily and frequently did knock over lockers. The women did not complain, being so used to them.

The other regulars were the rats who made use of the long shelf running around my office just below the low ceiling. They would be seen perfectly still looking at me with their red eyes, just watching. I took to trying to write poetry in order to concentrate my mind.

Sleeping during the day in a large hutment of forty or so sisters who were working all day, I was alone amongst all these empty rooms. There had been several robberies, of private possessions such as jewellery, money, all things to send back to the UK. Therefore I promised to listen for the intruder, deciding especially to keep awake after luncheon as the servants went off duty at two o'clock and absolutely no one was around, giving thieves hours of time safely to take what they wanted.

Getting into bed I listened and lo and behold there came a soft shuffle behind a partially hidden door which had a wardrobe in front of it exposing only the black latch. I kept very still with my eye on the latch and almost silently this lifted, the door opened a fraction, a black eye met mine and for an instant he seemed paralysed. Taking complete advantage I leapt out of bed, through another door and was right behind him giving chase in my nighty and bare feet all the time calling to the British on guard in the far end of the compound. They then took up the chase and finally caught him.

He was charged and the Indian law dealt with this case eventually. The Military Police and I had to appear for two days in the civil court. What a waste of time that was. He got off 'as he was only looking for a glass of water.' Someone had received a good bribe, no doubt putting him into further debt, as is the Indian's way of life, who have continuous loans with such high percentage hanging over them lifelong. This also gave me an insight into the manner of the civil courts; rows of such poor wretched people awaiting their cases to be heard by Indian Magistrates sitting on benches in a building in which cattle would be better housed in England.

Very soon I was given orders to go to a hospital in Ranchi by train via Calcutta. This was a three-day journey to Calcutta and then one day on. The train had the usual clamour with excitement from the travellers; everyone calling to an invisible person; porters laden like pack-horses with monstrous loads all competing over their colossal strength; they were all so thin and small, obviously very undernourished as children.

Reporting to the RTO (an Army Officer in charge of British personnel whenever they went by train) I was put into a first class carriage supplied with a fan, an essential factor for travelling over the very hot plains with intense dry winds of this vast country.

We stopped at stations en route for meals; many poor hungry people begging with their maimed children pushed towards you, so pathetic. The train staff shepherded passengers through the crowd into the dining rooms on the platform where a reasonably good meal was served always. The hot air was disturbed by a punka, a piece of cloth attached to the long plank hanging from the high ceiling controlled by a boy sitting on the floor with the long string attached to his big toe leading to the punka. By moving his toe up and down he could manage to swing this construction varying degrees, except when he fell asleep and was prodded by a passing waiter.

At night the train steward prepared our bunks. In the morning and throughout the day he served pots of tea nicely on a tray, with courtesy and good humour. Finally arriving in Calcutta with a great flourish; the noise predominating; the calling for porters, tea wallahs, food wallahs all calling their wares. The banging of doors, families greeting, all trying to be heard, to say nothing of the engines blowing off their volumes of steam.

I found the RTO, reporting my arrival. He informed me that I was to stay in the Army hostel until further orders, putting me in a car in which I was driven off.

Calcutta was a shattering place of contrasts, as all India is, but this even more so. Howrra Bridge, with its teeming millions crossing mainly towards the station, a sight never to be forgotten. At the station entrance was a high arch similar to Waterloo and the same size inside. On a later occasion there lay a dead body over which someone had the grace to place a sheet. Whole families literally in gutters, on pavements

The wealthy had large houses with delightful Indian architecture, many facades crumbling, surrounded with lawns. All extremes; very fat men with huge stomachs, then the starving little people, entirely depending on which caste they had the fortune or misfortune to be born into.

An aunt who had married a British officer in the Indian Army recounted an episode from the visit of the Prince of Wales to India in the early twenties or thirties. He was received with all pomp and ceremony that British India could produce. They were most capable of having the tact and experience of civil and military rule; all invitations, seating arrangements in correct order for a Royal Prince. All the Indian Royals and their entourages in fantastic coloured silks and jewels given their precedence of hierarchy, each caste his place, even down to the lowest untouchables.

This particular day, in Delhi I believe, took place on a huge parade ground with massed bands, a military display and colour of the many uniforms. Starting with the National

Anthem as the Prince arrived; speeches of welcome from notables.

Nearing the end before the final display, the Prince, taking every one by surprise and astonishment left his place and of course every one stood up. He walked onto the parade ground, his aides hurrying behind, across to the far end where the untouchables were and proceeded to shake hands with them. This was politically a bad move, according to general opinion and the aunt said she never forgave him! It was not protocol. No one knew why he had made this unusual gesture.

While enjoying my few days I heard that the hospital I was meant to go to was closing in any case. Deciding to ask for leave and permission to go to Darjeeling, as I was the right side of the country it would be easy. I made arrangements to go by train. This was some time before Hillary and Tensing of course and Everest had not been conquered; no one was climbing during wartime.

Taking the train towards the foothills with two engines puffing up the lower part and arriving at a unique small gauge railway to complete the journey to the foothills surrounded by huge snow-covered peaks disappearing into the clouds. It was such fun chugging up and up in this toy train. I stayed at the hostel that had a wide veranda from which there were great views. As the sun was going down the pinks and blues were magnificent and I shall always regret not accepting an offer of riding mules at 4am next day to see the sunrise.

There was some cheering and much laughter coming from the road behind the hostel and on going round I saw a gathering of children of all ages with happy faces and dressed in vivid blues, reds and yellows lining both sides of the rough road. It seemed ponies were being sent down this road at a great pace but having to slow somewhat at the slight bend just giving these children enough time to leap onto their backs and continue galloping down the hill. Great cheers and laughter until the next pony appeared. They were great people, so full of fun and daring.

Meeting another girl staying at the hostel we walked the surrounding country and villages enjoying the local people and finding they were everything the Gurkas are known for, their infectious happiness, primitive fun and helpless laughter for the slightest happening civilisation has robbed us.

In one Colonial style hotel where a good meal was served I met some army people on leave. As I was in uniform, compulsory in those days, the 'other ranks' were quite shy sometimes on approaching. So much of this discipline has broken down now, very good in certain ways only.

The week went by so quickly. Great luck in seeing Mount Everest in the early morning without cloud, seeming so close but obviously many miles away and up.

Returning to the toy railway was fun again. Calcutta and my orders to return to the 126 military hospital in Poona took the best part of a week. After reporting my return I was summoned to nurse a special case of a very sick soldier entirely during the day. He lay on a stretcher with his eyes closed, a deathly pallor and no response to touch, he was very ill indeed. Flies crawled all over his face, clustering into the corners of his mouth and eyes and crowing the encrusting dry lips. He made no movement to brush them away.

I had been sent to specialise this young man, bathing his face and sweat-soaked hair I proceeded to read the salient points of his notes. His wounds, it appeared were mostly on his buttock, a mass of shrapnel had penetrated into the bone causing a deep-seated infection oozing pus. He was so dehydrated that the primary job was to get some fluids into him. Managing to get him to take some fluids by mouth was an achievement. He had not so much as opened his eyes yet and really had no desire to do so.

Attending to his wounds was a major problem. The Colonel saw him when he visited the ward and simply said do what you can. Obviously he had to be turned in order to get to his wounds for estimating the damage and relieve the pressure. Without support from my medical superior I felt at a loss.

The next day my patient opened his eyes but was totally disinterested in anything. Not very encouraged I thought of some orthopaedic experience in the past when plaster casts were made full length for patients who had

44

tubercular bone infection. This was done in two halves in order to turn the patient whilst keeping the body rigid. I approached the Colonel and asked if this could be tried out, at least we could make the patient more comfortable in so doing.

This was approved and a request made to the orthopaedic department to come and measure him and discuss with me what was required. In the meantime I was giving all I could in nourishing liquids. I explained to the young man what we were going to do and at the same time impressed on him that this was common practice for certain cases, but if he became uncomfortable we would change. He seemed not to care about anything.

This was a large airy ward with approximately thirty beds. There were some patients who were convalescing and mobile whom I asked to help me in my efforts. I explained that two full-length casts were arriving but in order to be able to turn our patient I would need the help of five able-bodied men to help to do this three times a day. The front cast would first be placed on top and strapped to his body and gently, in a concerted movement, we would turn him over.

Volunteers were more than eager to help and in two days all was ready. With lots of cotton wool padding all over then the cast tied on it all worked wonderfully. The damage to his back was extensive and I hoped this provided some relief. He now took more interest in what was being done. All my duty time was devoted to him, with nourishing diet, turning, dressing him to break this barrier of silence. The rest of the chaps were now talking to him until soon he began to smile.

Eventually I won his confidence and slowly he talked, describing his terrible ordeal and multiple experiences of being blown up in his tank. Departure from Burma in his state was horrific, travelling over fearful roads, being passed like an unwanted parcel over thousands of miles from one hospital to another, onto trains, heat, flies, filth and stench from his untreated wounds. Gradually this awful story came out. He was only twenty and we both knew only a miracle could save him but it was good to let him talk.

In a while his response was amazing, becoming quite the cheeky chappy with his cockney humour. There was fun with the other boys who would do anything for him and who were a great help to me. After some weeks his face filled out, those hollow cheeks were no more. His contribution was his effort to get well enough to get back to England and see his parents and family. Deciding to make an appointment to see the Colonel to discuss the possibility of repatriation and possibly to fly, I was thinking of an officer with a mild amoebic dysentery who had been so lucky. But he had the backing of the General. This suggestion of mine seemed quite out of the question. Then persisting, 'Could it be by hospital ship, I would be happy to go with him?' This was as far as I dare go. Nevertheless I was angry as I felt 'they' were not really prepared to try.

In the meantime I was astonished to receive a gift from my helpers (instigated by my patient no doubt) of a cigarette case inscribed Poona '46. It is chromium-plated with an engraved design of horizontal patterns, slim for a lady's handbag. I was deeply touched and quite speechless, to think that they had gone to all that trouble, getting someone to go into town, having it inscribed and spending their hard-earned pay. I was quite inadequate in my thanks and when I look at it now I am filled with remorse at the terrible consequences that ensued.

In spite of my success with my bicycle one day I happened to take the corner into the gates of the hospital at speed. Picking myself up I realised my collarbone was damaged and it was extremely painful. After receiving treatment and being given a few days off I called on the ward to explain my predicament to my patient and the rest of the team with a little banter.

With my arm in a sling it took a long time to get dressed as it was so painful. I went with friends to meals to some of the good Indian restaurants, also to the Poona races, cheekily to see the elegant wealthy Indian ladies dressed in their graceful saris and exquisite jewellery. Such women were born into great wealth portraying dignity and great confidence. Always surrounded by family and friends they did not meet the outside world. The occasional official parties given by Indians were strictly men only.

Eventually recovering well enough to ride my transporter I went to visit the ward for news. There was quite a buzz; my team was full of news, asking me to look under my patient's bed. There lay all his kit, taken out of store and he was going on the next hospital ship for home in a day or so, hooray!

I was told officially to prepare to leave a day before in order to board the ship and that my patient would be brought down to Bombay by two orderlies. I made my farewells to the team and thanking them said to my lad, for that was all he was, 'I'll see you tomorrow.'

On my journey to Bombay I planned roughly what my routine would be on board ship. Fortunately I am a good sailor and have had a certain amount of experience on board. I could not help thinking it all a little strange that never once in three months did I see a matron or receive any suggestions from the Colonel. It had been medically a lonely endeavour.

Arriving at the station the scene was, as ever excitement combined with a great deal of shouting; porters answering demands from passengers to collect luggage and they coming at the double. There were memsahibs dressed in their colourful saris and as always wearing gold and jewellery, calling to coolies for assistance with bags. Always there were the tea boys in their slightly tarnished gold and red silk uniforms calling, 'Chai, chai' with tinkling little bells on top of the urns, adding to the great hubbub.

I found the RTO to report and receive instructions. I could hardly hear his quiet English voice above the clamber and not believing what I was hearing either proceeded to explain that I was meant for the hospital ship for the UK, my patient arriving next day. To my utter disbelief he informed me that the ship had sailed last night!

It was all a terrible let down for the patient. I was to report to another ship, knowing I was not to communicate with the hospital before leaving and I discovered I had joined another section bound for Singapore.

SAILING TO SINGAPORE

I met the twelve sisters on board with our matron who told us we were meant to be going to Hong Kong to board the POWs from Japanese prisons. At that time no one knew anything at all of their conditions or the slightest idea of their appalling imprisonment. This was a hospital ship and should be prepared for most normal medical conditions. Matron became a little carried away with the idea that this would be at the forefront of news giving a heroic homecoming to our troops. After this introduction we hardly saw her again for the whole journey. She informed us that she had become known as the Sister who had nursed Brigadier Orde Wingate through his bad pneumonia.

He was an exceedingly brave man who created and led long-range penetration troops known as the Chindits behind Japanese lines in the Burma jungle.

Leaving Bombay harbour quietly, for the first time without the fear of Japanese submarines was a strange but most welcome change, no convoy, lights without blackout, a new world. Although we had an almost empty ship we had been allocated the worst cabins I had ever occupied, especially to work. We were below the waterline, which meant no porthole, and air-conditioning on the blink that frequently broke down. With six in a small cabin and bunks so close there was no room to dress. In peacetime it would have been the cheapest cabin for one person.

Passing Ceylon brought back such good memories of that lovely country, now called Sri Lanka of course but so ruined by war.

Along the coast the ship slowed to a stop. All agog we saw landing craft making for us full of British soldiers wearing their red berets. This then was the 1st Para Brigade joining the ship - that should be good fun for us. Their destination was secret too and we enjoyed their company with no onerous duties.

One other naval officer was picked up a day or two later, the ship slowing down for him he managed to jump from the coastal vessel safely onto our ship. We eventually learnt that he was a secret authority on the Malay coast and in private consultation with Brigade officers. We had now turned down the Straits of Malacca. We were too far off to see the coast and to the best of our knowledge the Japanese might still be there.

Each day the whole of the ship's company listened to the BBC news, of which we were so starved. Up until now we had only the ship's daily bulletins with very limited items. But on the second day in the Straits it was announced that the 1st Para Brigade had safely landed on the coast of Malaya. Great cheers went up all around the deck, especially from the troops. The element that this would scare the enemy. Three days later we watched while the whole Brigade prepared to leave the ship fully equipped with huge loads on their backs and carrying arms of all descriptions to meet the enemy on the mainland at Port Swettenham.

It appeared no one knew what to expect, except a full-scale land battle. It was with some trepidation we watched them load themselves into the landing crafts and our prayers went with them. All were quite silent listening for firing or any kind of sounds across the water. We were too far away to see land except as a cloud in the distance. By the afternoon we suspected something was not normal and eventually we heard that they were returning to the ship.

Before sunset they had arrived in a dreadful state, covered from head to foot in mud, without any equipment at all, simply their lives. They were very quiet but eventually the story was told.

In spite of the most careful consultations with the naval authority on the Malay coast they had leapt out of the landing craft and simply sunk into soft mud about eight feet deep. They fought their way out of their heavy equipment to save their lives, arriving on the beach utterly exhausted and were revived by little Chinese children giving them coconut milk! How fortunate that there was no enemy.

Sailing on towards Singapore we first saw Sumatra on our right and later on our left the most appalling smell coming from Singapore. Now that we know the awfulness of conditions we can appreciate and marvel at the stoicism of the people coping with these awful Japanese. Worse still, how could Prince Philip allow himself to represent our country at the funeral of their Emperor while our people had up until then received not a penny of compensation for the inhuman treatment received from the Japanese?

The Brigade left immediately as we lay off port, we knew not where and we were told we would not be going ashore. There we remained while some high ranking officers in strange uniforms joined the ship and gave us bits of news of the Japs and how they had just melted away because of the American Bomb. We remained there a week in all during which time we were given orders to go ashore one evening to meet POWs who had come from a recuperation centre but we were told not to discuss their imprisonment! What a bizarre situation for everyone.

They were very shy and polite and we also found it difficult with somewhat stinted conversation, not knowing then anything of what they had experienced. There were no guidelines from our seniors, as we never saw Matron.

This was a very strange week of waiting, finally returning the way we had come, sailing up the Straits once more to Burma. In the Bay of Bengal the ship's doctor discovered a case of suspected rabies amongst the crew. Now we were stuck out in the Bay for days flying the yellow flag and awaiting the laboratory report. This is a very severe condition but fortunately it proved negative so with another lost week we arrived in Rangoon. Thankfully we were given permission to go into town after being cooped up for weeks. Two very surly and suspicious Rangoon officials came aboard and scrutinised our passports. They gave us a little very dirty local money, telling us its value and then they beetled off. We found the town dreary, the shops with the people unsmiling and suspicious and with nothing much to sell. Very soon we gladly returned to the ship thinking if that was communism we had seen enough – a depressed country.

Now we were told to be ready to receive patients and how thankful we were to be able to get back into a routine once more. Nothing was said by Matron of what to expect. According to gossip she was always swanning about on the top deck, having her cabin there, enjoying the company of retiring officers returning to the UK.

At last the patients arrived. They were mostly walking cases after having had a month's convalescence. There were a few women with a little girl with her mother who had a heart condition due to their appalling diet and conditions. Several of sisters spent our entire day at out patients' clinic dressing terrible leg ulcers, queues of men continuing throughout the day. There was no time to talk apart from polite enquiries regarding their health.

After a week It was time to alert someone of our bad conditions, where we snatched at meals with never a moment to breathe fresh air on deck, plus our cramped cabins in the tropical heat, waking at night bathed in sweat when the air-conditioning failed.

Two of the sisters had heard of a matron on board who was returning to the UK on sick leave after having experienced a long and difficult time in Burma. We decided to appeal to her to arrange better conditions for us. She admitted it would be difficult for her to take over command but she understood our predicament. Without delay she gave us regular duty hours and meal times. Several of us found a quiet corner to sleep and eat on deck and what a relief that was. Sometimes we sat on deck with some of the patients who were amusing and made light conversation, not having lost their sense of humour in spite of all they had endured.

Passing along the coast towards Ceylon once more the ship slowed down to receive mail. This as you can imagine was the lifeline for every one of our passengers. Direct news from home was the most precious item for most. Of course there were the acute disappointments and this could be worrying for us all. There was sadness, with bereavements, homes lost in bombing, wives who had not waited – this was very hard to bear and here we came into the picture slightly as they sometimes threatened suicide. It was hard for their friends to have to arrange never to leave them on their own and we too had to watch them. We all felt something of anger towards these selfish wives.

Sailing through the Indian Ocean each day meant nearer to home and the POWs began to believe this. There was gaiety in the air and there was the prospect of going through Suez for the first time since war began. It is always an incongruous sight to find camels walking over a wall of sand so close to one and seeming to be on a level with the top deck of a big ship and somehow one keeps thinking it must be unreal. There we were in amongst other ships that had been queuing at the entrance and slowly making our way through the two deserts. Arriving at Port Said always meant trading for the Egyptians with a lot of fun for the passengers with baskets of goods being sent up to them by rope and after a great deal of haggling and teasing the purchase money being placed in the baskets and lowered to the traders in the bum boats. There being several of these boats surrounding the ship much business was done to the delight of the Egyptians as they had had no trade due to the war and the lack of pleasure steamers passing through the canal.

Out into the Mediterranean there was a slight hint of climate change as we approached the Rock of Gibraltar. It was now December and the Atlantic was rough and became much worse with a force ten gale in the Bay of Biscay. Life style changed with the crew in their navy blues and after much delving into old luggage from the hold we retrieved musty and damp grey uniforms smelling to high heaven, not having been worn since 1943. Into the English Channel, passing the Isle of Wight the sea was more regular. Into Southampton Water and England at last for all these wonderful people.

Except for the relatives there was no welcome. Surely they could have produced someone official. We were told to get them ashore as quickly as possible with the Captain dispensing with all formalities. Leaning over the rail I watched a family receive their son and was told the father had been a prisoner with the Nazis and now both were free at last.

But all was so silent, except from the relatives there was not a cheer, not a band, nothing. Already they were the Forgotten Army.

This is the way it has always been with England. Once you have lost your usefulness you are put away in a closed cupboard and forgotten. As a nation we are slow to realise, but at last there are rumblings for the acknowledgement of women's great contribution towards winning the war but that has taken sixty years.

England

I was given leave and went to stay with my sister and family who were still in North Wales. I travelled on the night train arriving at three o'clock in the morning but decided not to disturb them so I stayed until six o'clock in the station waiting room where there was a cosy fire. Of course they were amazed at me being there after all these years and for not ringing sooner but I felt to return in daylight would be less troublesome.

1947 was the coldest, most miserable time that the country had ever known. My poor sister with two young children was finding it so hard to have sufficient food – one small lump of coal for two days. I found it particularly hard to bear after the tropics, suffering so badly from chilblains from knees to toes. The doctor suggested I stay in bed. After ten days I was posted to Netley Military Hospital outside Southampton.

It was wet, cold and grey and for these first days quite miserable. Not knowing the area I longed to be back in the sun. I wondered how soon I could return to the warmth and colour again.

Netley was a monolithic Victorian building, three storeys high. Three corridors were straight and each a quarter of a mile long with broad arched windows from floor to ceiling. I was in charge of the top floor while on night duty with a sister each on the lower floors. One particular night warning of a severe frost was sent to each sister so that we had to make sure all windows were closed and locked. The corridor windows had two iron bars across top and bottom, which took two orderlies to manipulate. Finally the military police came to check it all.

At midnight I joined the other two for dinner and on walking along the corridor I was amazed to see one window half open and still moving and calling the orderly we closed it together. Arriving downstairs I was all agog to tell the others of this incident when I noticed a commotion happening on the ground floor. The sisters were involved with feeding the head orderly with sips of brandy to bring him round from a faint. Evidently he had been faced by the ghost of a nurse of the first war by the description of the uniform. The sister told us she could hardly keep a straight face as the orderly was a tough fellow who normally kept the young orderlies enthralled with his brave escapades in the parachute regiment. Later on we discovered that a nurse had committed suicide by jumping from the top floor window, unable to face the disgrace, in those days, of her pregnancy.

To my delight after a few weeks I was posted back to India. I never knew how these things happened but I could not wait to get to Port Said and to feel the sun on my back. My poor sister and her family made me feel so guilty.

There again was the great arch, the Gateway to India with the usual noise, colour, heat, and flies and rich and poor destitute people. But there was a mystery about both the country and people. I was back in Poona once more. Now there was the question of should I be thinking of staying in the Army or demob. Africa was my first love or should I choose to take a course at the Tropical Diseases Hospital. There was lots of time to think about that now.

Eventually I returned to England and left the Army, sadly in some ways. But as our Colonial Service was on the cards for liquidation in the hands of left wing politicians I would have to make my choice for the future.

Applying to the Tropical Disease Hospital, in Marylebone at that time, I was accepted for the year's course. This would improve my knowledge of diseases I had already encountered.

There were several newly trained nurses doing the course who were quite fun. Matron was the kindest I had ever met up with and she gave us every opportunity to enjoy the theatres, getting us free tickets and allowing us to return late from matinées if the timing overran our duty times – very flexible. All the staff had meals together, doctors, nurses and laboratory staff with Matron at the head of the table. She kept the conversation lively with some unlikely topics but shoptalk was frowned upon.

Lectures were given by Sir Philip Manson Barr whose father-in-law, Professor Manson allegedly discovered the connection between the bite of the female anophelese mosquito and malaria disease. We were given amusing anecdotes of the behaviour of some of the old professors of the nineteenth century when they wore wigs to dinners and the ladies sitting next to them could observe lice wandering over their wigs. Also their personal hygiene was questionable and daily baths were not in vogue. All this information and much more came from his mother-in-law. Thankfully times have changed. We enjoyed all the lectures from these charming men.

Professor Hamilton Fairley, an Australian is famous for inventing Mepacrine that must have saved the lives of thousands of troops fighting in the Burmese jungle and the Far East. I remember vividly literally having to put the tablet on the tongue of each man as they stubbornly resisted taking them to begin with. It eventually made them a bit yellow but that was all. A stubborn Englishman can be the most trying chap.

Later on Professor Hamilton Fairley's son, also a doctor, was killed by the dreadful IRA for no reason, an innocent man. The patients were interesting. Usually from the tropics the men were sometimes eminent men in their sphere. Some women were there too for investigation.

It was particularly nice and a great treat to be near all the wonderful shops though we were severely restricted by coupons. After a year passed and we had passed our exams matron asked me to stay another six months and put me in charge of a ward for holiday relief work.

Afterwards not getting into Africa it was made easy for me to accept a post with BP in Iran.

PERSIA

Arrangements were made by the British Petroleum Company for me to be given a post in their nursing service in Iran. Instructions were sent to me to go by flying boat from Poole Harbour. I was to go to an hotel in London and join a few men who were returning to Iran from leave.

The weather was bitterly cold, with snow forecast. I registered and found the hotel comfortable. My instructions were to expect a taxi at 4am. I noticed some men in the dining room and assumed they might me the four passengers who were to be my travelling companions.

Hardly sleeping, I was awake for my call and looking forward to the new experience of the flying boat. There was not a sound to be heard. London was unusually silent. Opening my curtain I saw thick snow lying deep – now what would we do?

All was resolved when one of the men explained that a snowplough was going ahead of the car all the way to Poole. There was no heating in cars in those days (how spoiled we are now). I was so glad of my fur coat and fur muff.

The first day's flight was so cold, with again no heating. I put my feet into my muff, hoping the sunshine would penetrate through the window. We were heading for Sicily in eight hours' flying, arriving about four o'clock. The landing was so smooth and with the opening of the plane's door the balmy air came into the cabin carrying along with it the scents of thyme, sage, mint and herbs, the heralds of spring. The Mediterranean air was a great contrast from England.

The hotel with marble floors was a joy. The anticipation of a hot bath and Italian dinner was a nice thought. Off again in the morning, next stop Cairo. How different from wartime, knowing where one was going.

Landing on the Nile, with winter sunshine and comfortable warmth (away now with fur). Cairo - a noisy

56

place, motor horns blaring for the slightest excuse, crowded pavements with cafés; everyone talking and greeting friends on the opposite side of the road, crossing over in front of traffic regardless; the Arabs' voluminous jelebas flying up with the gusts of passing traffic.

There were totally veiled women wearing visors of thickly crocheted lace, which they could see through and others with the usual black duella with hood. The Moslem religion, in my opinion, subjects women to so much cruel domination by the males.

Arriving at Shepherds Hotel by afternoon one of our party suggested we might have time to get to the pyramids. But by the time we had confirmed our reservation and had tea we realised we could run over curfew. In any case after sundown the desert became bitterly cold.

The hotel was full, teeming with many nationalities. There were wealthy Egyptians, wearing expensive cream suits, with the red fez, the mobile black tassel seeming to emphasise the positive assertion in their conversation. Also present were British army and naval officers and Turkish uniformed officials. I could imagine all the intrigue that was happening in Cairo, at that time the political centre of the universe. In the aftermath of the upheaval of the war the special services were there, trying to stabilise business and secure some normality. A wonderful background for writers of spy stories!

Away again next morning, heading for Basrah in Iraq. We landed on Lake Hamina and were taken to an old Arab hotel with an arcade of Romanesque arches. This I became familiar with over three years. There we awaited a couple of cars that would take us across the desert and our destination, Abadan.

The climate was at its best in winter as this was far south, on the Persian Gulf. It was the terminus for oil tankers and this was the refinery distributing centre. It was a huge organisation by BP.

I was accommodated in Abadan for a few days before being sent up to Fields, to a small hospital. Flying in a small Cessna 'plane over the volcanic mountains and looking down I saw thousands of miles of sharp points as though an immense eruption had turned the land upside down. It was no place to travel by road. I could see clearly the oil derricks where the oil was extracted from the chalky ground.

Arriving at Masjid-i-Suleymân I was taken to the Nurses Home and was met with a friendly welcome and taken to my room. It was pleasant with all mod cons. There was a communal dining room and sitting room for the staff. I met them all by degrees. They were all affable but clannish Scots, the young matron, the doctors and six or seven sisters. I was critical, but a little weary of Scotland and did privately hope they would leave it at home sometimes. I was not truly accepted by them, regardless of my friendly efforts.

The hospital was small, old and inadequate, built in the previous century. There were some native wards with beds much too close and hardly any room for screens. It was almost impossible to find room when their families came, preparing food for the patient on the floor, as was their custom.

The employees had far better accommodation. There were two private wards for maternity. Being a general hospital they were prepare to accept all patients. Three extreme cases impressed my memory, an Indian lady who had not the slightest pain during the birth of her first baby! Wonderful; while another maternity case was brought in unable to give birth after having been in labour for three days in her village and then travelling for another three on the back of a donkey!

On examination the doctor found a very distended bladder was preventing the birth. On expelling this the baby was found to be dead. This then called for a serious removal of the child, bringing it away in sections with me giving anaesthetic by mask and drip, a primitive method with very little room to perform. The poor doctor had to do this grizzly operation to save the mother's life. I did admire him. It was a horrible task. The lady recovered well from these extreme measures. What amazing stamina these primitive people have.

The third case was of a man who had been bitten by an animal with rabies and developed hydrophobia. It is the most terrible disease to witness and we were not to nurse him. Instead it was arranged for special orderlies to attend to him. There was no accommodation for such a severe disease, which can be transmitted by the patient's saliva, and the virus enters via the wound under the skin. This gives signs of throat restriction and severe madness and in his raving madness he develops a great instinct to bite anyone. It was a very distressing sight to behold. My tropical diseases course had described the symptoms but I had never witnessed it until now. Without an isolation ward he had to be put in a tiny room with bars, it was awful.

By reading of the work that had been started by the Shah's sister in some of the primitive villages in Persia I discovered how incredibly tough the people were. They had nothing in their communities to support them. Miles from anywhere; no sanitation; no clean water; scratching the soil for food. With no clinics; no doctors; absolutely nothing but the harsh landscape. I feel sure it is the same today.

In this area we were very well provided for by the Company. It was all very efficient with a friendly atmosphere. The housing was good with all needs met. The Company also arranged weekly entertainment.

There was an excellent bazaar where wonderful crafts of all kinds could be bought at reasonable cost, in fact would be much prized by today's standards. I found excellent tailoring, which I was able to wear in London.

The hills around us were quite high and rugged. There were reports of some wild animals that were rarely seen, with the exception of snakes, some of them were krites, deadliest of all as there is no antidote. One night the night watchman killed two adults and six of their offspring. As far as I know there is still no cure, with death within fifteen minutes.

For seven months of the year it was intensely hot, but from November to March it was very pleasant. As we were so far south it snowed only one day which was around mid-December.

Sometimes a party of us would picnic some miles out in the country by a pure clean stream that would be flowing in January and February. There would be fields of tulips as far as the eye could see, the next time anemones of blue and the next time red anemones in their millions and grape hyacinths so huge they would leave a horticulturist baffled. All their roots went down a considerable way into the ground to withstand the intense heat of the summer months.

By now I had met my charming husband, Donald, and in June had gone home to prepare for our wedding. For convenience we were being married in London. We returned to a sweet house, everything supplied by the Company down to the last teaspoon. I was no longer allowed to work, as that was a general condition in every service in those days.

Most people slept in their gardens in summer but in the hills where we were the heat hardly altered only there was no sun beating down. I was so fortunate to have a wonderful servant called Hiada and a small boy from the Bachtiar Tribe whom we called M'toto. They cleaned and cooked and came with us on our trips into the country to cook and help with the tents. They enjoyed these times.

Sometimes at night and long before dawn one heard, in the far distance the sound of tinkling camel bells coming from the hills. A caravan of seventy or so approaching silhouetted against the sky as dawn was breaking. They came from the north with all the men, women and children of their tribe, the men riding the camels and the women walking carrying babies! This was typical as women were regarded as livestock.

This was a regular wintertime trade for their excellent work in their arts and crafts, of infinite variety. There were tempting buys of silks, silver, ivories, pictures, carpets and many more beautiful things. They usually stayed for about three days for displaying and selling. Loading up their camels once more they trekked to their next destination which was Abadan. We bought carpets of course and pictures by Deamon and still enjoy them today.

All employees of the Company took Friday as their day off as we were in a Moslem country, their religion being strict as it still is today. Unfortunately some of their leaders became politically destructive which proved extremely sad for their country and their economy. A man, some may remember, called Mossadeck forbade any employee to travel within the country to visit any of the ancient cities that we longed to see. He spent his time in bed, finally stirring up terrible political opposition to the Shah and his family and eventually removing them. This madness reverberated throughout the whole Company. The power of the fanatical Mullahs made it unsafe in the bazaars where Britons were murdered in Abadan.

This is where I had come to live, very happily and I had a beautiful baby girl, Susan. Eight thousand employees, Donald and I amongst them, were now disbanded and sent home indefinitely on full salary until a decision about us all was made.

It was a tragedy for this fine Company, for the employees and for the Iranians, thousands of whom had been given a good living for the first time in their lives. The whole stricture reflected a turbulence in the country from which I believe it will never recover as a result of their fundamental attitude to their religion.

RETURN TO KENYA

We lived with Granny for a year. She very kindly put up with us all, and eventually our dog Lila when she came out of the horrible kennels, that awful penance that all animals endured. Medstead Manor was a large house with one hundred acres and a home farm in a tiny village near Alton in Hampshire.

Due to the trouble in Persia we had felt it safer to send my darling baby home with her English nanny to Granny. I could hardly bear the waiting until I got back to hold her again. She was just one year old. Arriving in England and getting to Granny's house I opened the hall door and there she was walking towards the nursery but turning she saw me and cried, 'Mummy.' I never wanted us to be parted ever again.

After waiting a year Donald was tired of the uncertainty and considered buying a farm in Africa as opposed to England as one required greater capital here. I eventually persuaded him simply to manage a farm for a year before laying out our capital. Nevertheless we had to make many decisions and I could never quite understand why D. could not have bought a small cottage for us to secure our return if it became necessary. But life was a puzzle in our upset world. I did insist that we should go together, no more parting, and have my second baby out there. This was 1952.

We sailed on the SS Kenya on her maiden voyage, a lovely trip on a new ship. I was back again at Port Said with the sunshine. At Aden there was a British gunboat. Evidently a certain amount of trouble was brewing in the Gulf there. The sea was so placid, like a mirror and yet a strange heaving movement under the surface was making people rather ill. I found it the strangest movement I had ever experienced. It left one's head floating about detached from the body.

After a day or two taking on oil and water and supplies and learning whether we would be permitted by the gunboat to continue our journey we were away once more. How glad we were to get out of the sticky heat of Aden.

Sailing down the coast of Africa brought back memories of Somalia and the millions of miles across this vast land. Although I had travelled thousands of miles of it I had, in fact only had a minute glimpse by comparison.

Mombasa would be the next stop. I was hoping I could remember some useful Swahili. There was the usual documentation and customs to go through. We had even brought our dear little dachshund Lila, as Granny could not keep her. I thought she would have loved her. Her own Becky was very old and Lila had wonderful games with the white Persian cats. But in any case my dear little Sue and Lila were great friends and we loved her.

Donald had bought a paper to read on the train and while reading he asked me what is Mau Mau? I had never heard of it and never gave it a second thought.

We all got on the same train I had travelled in years ago. We were going to Thompsons Falls Hotel to stay a night before going on to the farm we had arranged to manage while the German owner was away for six months. Next day D. went to introduce himself. It appeared that the husband had already departed and the wife was all ready to go too, not allowing any time for details to be discussed.

It was a mixed farm with hundreds of acres and sixty African employees plus two mastiff dogs. Next day the wife gave us the minutest cottage and a very poor welcome. All instructions seemed to have been in writing with a great deal for D. to study. She was departing as soon as she could, which later made me wonder how much she knew of the situation regarding the Mau Mau.

The first night we wondered how we were going to live in this one small room. It was very poor but we finally settled in somehow! At 4am we were disturbed by the arrival of the police. D. went outside to meet them and after some time came in to report that the police had rounded up forty of our employees as Mau Mau. This name again which no one seemed to think at all serious.

As soon as he was able D. went to the nearest farm owned by an Englishman to enquire what all this was about. He told him not to be concerned as it was but a Kikuyu tribal upset. Within two weeks the first British murders occurred just two miles from us.

All this was difficult to understand and was indeed alarming. Evidently, in spite of many warnings the Governor of the Colony had not taken the information seriously, or perhaps could not handle it as he was nearing retirement, in the hope that the new Governor could deal with it. This then was the general opinion ultimately.

The whole trouble blew up into a disaster and even today has simply made room for evil Dictators to take their ill judgements and destroy each country, lining their own pockets and that of their cronies.

Kenyatta was carrying out these evil rituals in our own forests. The poor employees on the farms were being forced into taking the foul oaths, swearing to kill the owners of the farms, mostly British, for whom they had worked since they were children, serving happily and loyally.

This is exactly what is now happening in Zimbabwe, such a tragedy for a wonderful country. The African is between the devil and the deep blue sea.

We finished our six months with that farm and proposed to care for a second one in order to complete the year, which I had promised Donald we would do. But it was becoming more obvious that our plan to buy out here was much too insecure. I went to Nairobi with Susan to await the birth of Kate. This was another grievous time when she was kept downstairs away from me, a cruel rule of which I was not aware. I suffered much and she too. Kate took a long time to arrive and I was beside myself with worry. A most dreadful time.

When I returned to the farm we were given the opportunity to carry pistols. Many more murders had taken place and things had become serious. I seemed to have missed the allocation for a pistol but a kind relative heard and sent me one from England. Frequent raids were made by the local defence in our forests. There was little we could do, except bring our employees out of the forest to around the farmhouse for their protection.

We put barbed wire thickly all round the house and kept the twelve bore shot gun under the bed and had a hole cut in the ceiling as an emergency place to hide the children in dire circumstances.

I had had enough, although D. wanted to stay and be awfully 'British'. I fully realised that there was a limit and we would never buy a farm. Each night we moved out to an English couple's home who kindly accommodated several people and we slept communally. We were all advised to do this, bringing all valuables such as passports and chequebooks.

Six months previously I had come to the conclusion that Africans, both men and women needed some medical help locally. I had started a small clinic where they could come to ask for advice each morning at ten o'clock when I could treat small wounds. This was much appreciated by them and for serious cases I took them into the native hospital thirty miles away. I found there was a great neglect on some of the farms, probably as much from ignorance as anything else. Sometimes they would ask me to come down to their huts for a difficult birth, which may have been true or merely a ruse. One took a chance.

There were alarming times when there appeared to be an attack and D. would be down with the cattle. I would see something happening and phone for help to the number given for emergencies but the African at the other end would pretend not to understand.

The British farmers had formed a small defence unit, meeting in our farm as most of the forest on our land was the Mau Mau headquarters, with Kenyatta there. At one time one of his runners was caught and on him was found a death list of the British farmers. We were told of this but apparently our name was not included. People appeared to want to know the reason but we had no idea. I did not pay any attention to it. It was only after I returned home that it slowly dawned on me that it may have been that my innocent little clinic had some influence in this.

Certain of the wives were not approving of my action, but good came of it knowing the Africans were badly needing it. Several times I took them in my car to the native hospital where they were well treated. I had a call to go to

65

the huts to see a girl who had had a baby but had retained the placenta or afterbirth. There she was sitting on the floor with the cord trailing in the dirt. She was looking very well. The two midwives were there, old and without any cleanliness whatsoever, but that was what it was like. I asked them to bring her to my car. I took her and one old woman to Nakura Hospital. Saying goodbye I hastily went to snatch a little shopping and before I was done there was the young mother calling 'Mem Sahib,' happily waving to me. They must have been well endowed with antibodies!

Sometimes we would go to see the millions of flamingos, their legs so very pink against the blue water of the glorious sulphur lake at Nakura. On our return we would picnic overlooking the great crater of the Rift Valley, teeming with game so well known today by tourists but no one but us there in those days.

Having had anxious letters from home from those who were worried about us, especially D.'s aunt who had great sympathy for our situation. She had had a similar experience in the First World War, being left on her own with many acres and a hundred Africans working on the farm, with her husband away fighting. I had asked her to look for a small cottage for us to come back to. Writing by return she offered us one of her cottages as the tenant had only that morning given notice. It was for us if we cared to have it. I replied by return and started to make arrangements.

Although we both disliked giving in we knew there was no future here, with a dicey government and of course later Kenyatta became President of Kenya, virtually a dictator.

Arriving back in England, thankfully but with D. jobless, we settled down gratefully in the delightful cottage in Rudgwick in Sussex. After we had dressed on the first morning my dear two year old said, 'Mummy you have forgotten your gun.'

Some six months went by and D. found out that a company called Seismograph had been wanting him to work in their headquarters in Kent on the North Downs which was a perfect small village. Eventually we found a big old house to rent with twenty acres and only a mile down the road from the office.

This is where our third daughter, Joanna was born and all three had a happy life here, amongst the animals with the garden and security. The village was Downe where Darwin had lived and his house is now a famous museum which people come from all over the world come to see. Our house had been occupied for many years by Darwin's nephew, also a very learned scion of the family. The house was part Elizabethan, Regency and Victorian. We loved it, working quite hard to restore it and the land, which we used for breeding children's ponies, with some cows and sheep to improve the condition of the pasture. This was a delightful home for fifteen years when Donald's retirement was approaching.

Looking back I consider, in spite of all our somewhat turbulent life how fortunate we were up to that date.

OPEN HOUSE

To have water in the form of a small lake is a bonus to any property, for several pleasures. Apart from the action of the wind on water, ever reflecting the sky, sunrises and sunsets, flight of birds, but to us our greatest pleasure is observing the daily life of the water birds.

Two Aylesbury ducks had established themselves before we arrived on the scene and a small mallard with a damaged wing made up the trio of inseparable friends.

Making friends with us was fairly easy, as food in winter is an attractive and popular asset so that eventually they came when called and in due course accepted corn from my hand.

As local duck gossip penetrated the feathered communities other mallard arrived, the family growing in numbers and varieties.

We gave the name of Jason to the Aylesbury as he led the fleet! He inspected all new arrivals meticulously, leading his fleet across the water with ever widening streaks of Vs stretching over the surface in fascinating patterns.

Being conspicuously white we felt he was in danger from Renard. In a short time Mrs Jason became our first casualty, which saddened us all. On inspection we thought it *was* the fox. The duck escape mechanism is too slow, with heavy body to lift into the air.

Nevertheless our bird population continued to increase, now including tufted duck, several pairs of moorhen, geese, both Brent and Canadian, the latter producing six young hatched in safety on the island on the lake. Coots, swans, tufted duck and always more and more mallard kept arriving.

We built four more waterfall ponds in our garden and several mallard flew in to visit them, making precise landings, ducking under the water, bottoms up with great splashings.

A pair of moorhens took up permanent residence, making a cosy well-hidden nest amongst the 'Ladies garters' and sitting hard they produced one egg daily. The sitting was a shared arrangement from devoted parents. This continues today after twelve years and against all hazards. But they do not tolerate even other young to enter their pond and with their three long claws will hold the intruder under the water and drown it.

Breeding time began with the mallard becoming magnificent in their psychedelic greens, blues and various brown markings, helped no doubt by our complementary feeding. There was ferocious pecking and fights, a particularly brutal time for females who were raped by six or more drakes day after day. This is a sad reflection on certain male species including humans, to our utter shame.

Dropwing now became a devoted companion to Jason but neither could fly. Instead they did a very hasty waddle so similar to a long distance walker as in the Olympics.

All new borns were into the water only moments after breaking the shell with parents hovering. Bobbing about through the reeds on the rippling water, but one squeak from mother and instant obedience. The discipline was remarkable.

Apart from the water birds pheasant and partridge still came pecking about the garden through the hedge from the rough grass outside. Oscar was cock pheasant, becoming a particular friend. He took to visiting us coming into the greenhouse at first and sometimes the sitting room quite unafraid, gently pecking seed out of my hand. Sadly suddenly he stopped and we suspected the horrid guns somewhere. One day Mrs Oscar appeared in my sitting room bringing her four chicks with her, alarming a visitor who had rather a shock and was probably disapproving of our eccentricity.

The barn owl often appeared as the sun went down and sat on the post in our garden, so handsome, swivelling his head in almost a complete circle inspecting the area from his lookout. Then without any warning spreading out his great wings with their exquisite markings and lifting into the air eyeing the ground, seeing his target and diving down like an arrow to the ground.

The mallard balls of fluff would number as many as sixteen or so but with constant exposure to birds of prey and rats very few would survive. This is surely Tennyson's, 'Nature red in tooth and claw.'

I had often noticed how careless mallard mothers in particular were. One day having arrived in our garden the hen realised two chicks were missing and from the penetrating squeaks of these minute creatures struggling through the long grass it might have seemed like a huge forest to them. Mother in some agitation gathered together the rest in a tight ball telling them not to move a feather. They remained exactly while she went to the rescue of the two in distress. I watched in admiration, the discipline impressive, not a single movement made by the furry cushion. On another occasion a mother left her cushion of fluff and never returned. In the end we managed to capture them with some effort and put them under a broody hen and they grew into fine ducklings.

In the meantime our 'ladies garter' moorhens hatched, one each day a pure black fluff with long legs and three dangerous claws. From day one they could out-race any of the others.

Swans circling overhead gave notice of their arrival. We watched their spectacular landings as the great yellow feet spread out. Heels down cutting into the surface of the mirror-like water, creating a bow wave and landing their heavy bodies with such grace. The take-off was equally dramatic, enormous outstretched wings flapping, a fast paddle, a loud squawk and up and away lifting themselves into the air, circling around the lake and the pair would be on their way.

Another tragedy alas awaited us. The pen returning with the cob flew into the electric cable in the nearby field. We could see she was in trouble and Donald found her with deep lacerations across her chest. In spite of our attempts and inspection by the vet nothing seemed possible. She died in the lake, all intensely sad as we watched the cob in attendance over her for two days. It was necessary for him to have his mourning. Afterwards we buried her. She was a young bird still having her brown feathers. That was the end of the swans, the cob never returning or any other swans ever coming again.

Our little ponds soon became a popular rendezvous for our feathered friends and would soon fill up with gossiping mallard. This always reminded me of the women from an African village doing their washing in the stream or perhaps market day; much chatter, gossip, noise, laughter and joy.

When the rest of the ladies failed to appear we realised that egg laying was in progress and in due course the first sightings of the hatchlings appeared. Great interest was taken by all the males who wanted a closer look. Our household were just as curious with everyone counting and shouts of, 'There's another one, I can see another' or, 'That makes twelve' etc.

It amazed us the immense amount of exercise these newly hatched chicks endured from the mother. No consideration was given to the rough terrain plus the speed that these dear little balls of fluff had to cope with in order to keep up with mother. It was unbelievable.

Needless to say intense interest was created by all the community but they were only permitted at a certain distance or mamma would rush them. When she brought them up to the lawn we gave them some very fine corn, suitable for the young but mamma would never feed with them, just watched her brood with aggressive warnings to the rest of the community, while her babies fed avidly.

Another family we were so fond of was the little owls but now sadly the builders have removed their habitat. It was such a pleasure to watch both parents trying to encourage a nervous owlet to take its first flight. Once it took five hours to achieve this! He had to walk up the rough stones leading to the peak that once supported the roof of the old barn. The timid youngster took a considerable time with much calling from the parents. He reached the desired place where there was a gap of approximately two yards. It was getting dark and I was hoping he would hurry up. My heart went out to the parents of this backward baby who did finally take the plunge. Hooray!

Day and night they called to each other, such a racket, plus the bats with their squeaks, nevertheless they were great company especially if one could not sleep.

In season there are flights of linnets, greenfinches with their distinctive call of squeezzzzzh and lovely flashes of green and yellow. When we started the garden we had to grow hedges to encourage the nesting of birds. Blackbirds, thrushes, tits, finches and all the usual garden birds eventually took up residence.

One spring morning it was a lovely surprise to find a hoopoe gracing the lawn. He stayed for three days. I notified the local birdwatchers' club but the message was never passed on.

In 1994 the first Canada geese arrived to inspect the lake and must have found it to their liking as they are still here in 2001, breeding on the island with three or four babies each year. They are wonderful parents as well disciplined as all the rest. At the first hatching I won a small battle with my husband, not allowing them into the garden again. On their first visit they brought their four handsome chicks to see us. With twelve great feet over our small lawn, plus the usual mess I had to do something. I laid down a roll of green plastic netting from their particular entrance. This they did not like at all. From that day to this they have never attempted to bring any of their broods into the garden. I think this is remarkable as they come each year to have their chicks with each brood never attempting to enter. They grow well and by August they are taught to fly in short bursts with much flapping of their great wings. They are given their practice flights on the water daily to begin with followed by circling over the lake and eventually off to visit friends and relations. All families born here return regularly, to begin with every Monday morning arriving before dawn with great honkings. I have seen as many as seventy at one time, almost filling the lake.

Although the Isle of Wight is famous for the red squirrel only once has one been seen in our garden. I blame the 'shoot' which is in the wood a little distance from the house.

When visitors call they can be quite startled by a sudden flight of mallard flying over our sitting room in order to get to the lake and the sudden whirr of wings almost make them duck their heads, forgive the pun!

Later in the year the big moult begins. With their loss of feathers they lose their glorious colour. The pheasant loses his long tail feathers and I have noticed how nervous they become as though they are somewhat alarmed at their condition.

After Christmas it all starts again and we keep Open House.